QUEEN MARY 2

*The Greatest Ocean Liner
of Our Time*

QUEEN

MARY 2

The Greatest Ocean Liner
of Our Time

John Maxtone-Graham

photography by Harvey Lloyd

with contributions from Michel Verdure and Yves Guillotin

Bulfinch Press
New York • Boston

Bulfinch Press
Time Warner Book Group
1271 Avenue of the Americas
New York, NY 10020
Visit our Web site at www.bulfinchpress.com

Produced by Carpe Diem Books

First Edition

ISBN 0-8212-2885-4
Library of Congress Control Number 2003116444

Book design by Reynolds/Wulf Design, Inc.

Printed in Hong Kong

Page 4–5: Under way at sea for the first time, *Queen Mary 2* cuts a fine maritime figure in late September 2003. *Opposite:* One of the vessel's four revolutionary Mermaid pods, complete with burnished, stainless steel propeller, comes in for a landing before installation. *Overleaf: Queen Mary 2*'s construction starts early on a foggy morning in Forme B. *Page 10*: Barbara Broekman's tapestry portrait of *Queen Mary 2* in New York dominates the Brittania Restaurant. Appropriately, the captain's table is positioned directly beneath it. (© MICHEL VERDURE)

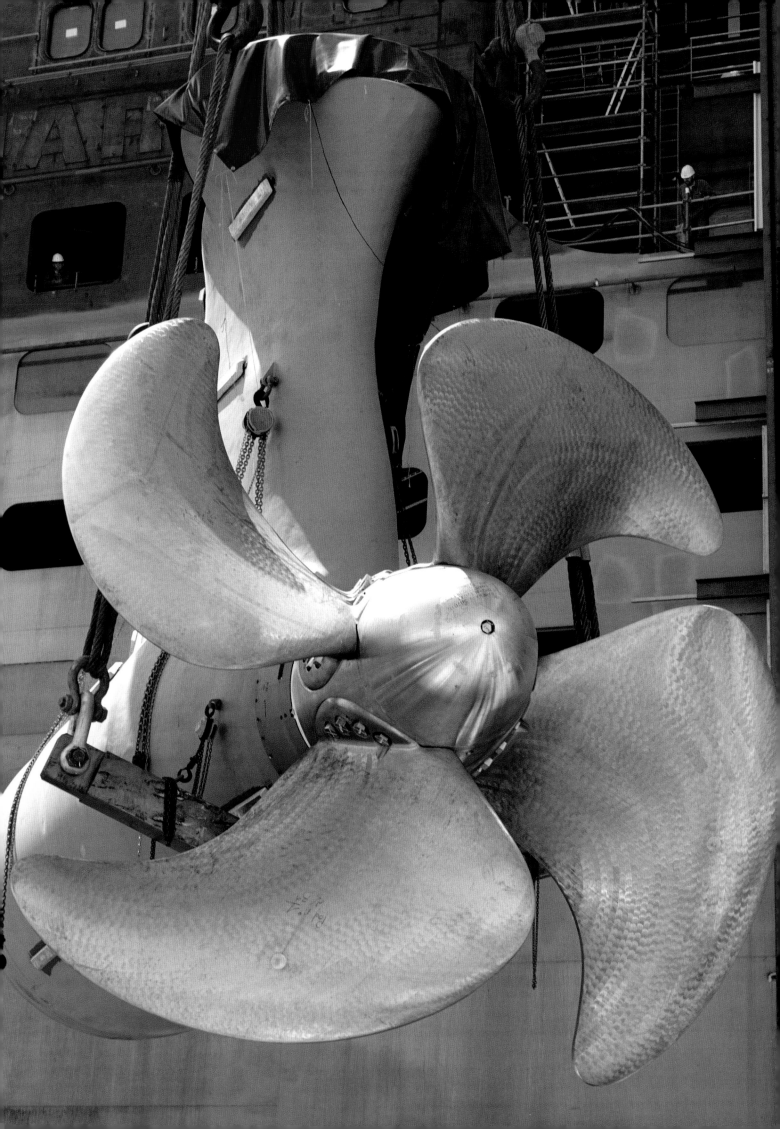

Contents

Preface

This is the third Cunard history I have undertaken and, because of its extraordinary *raison d'être*, surely the most rewarding. The launch of the world's largest ocean liner at the start of the twenty-first century demands fullest documentation no less than admiration. *Queen Mary 2* is an incredible one-of-a-kind, a vessel to warm the hearts of every maritime historian and passenger alike. In shipyard lingo, "newbuilding" describes any ship under construction; this latest Cunard ocean liner embodies newbuilding of incomparable significance.

Of all contemporary cruise lines, Cunard boasts the most profound Anglo/American links. Founded by a Canadian, the Line and its steamers have served as palpable maritime connectors for 164 years, uniting mother country with former colony, the burgeoning, boisterous, and prosperous United States. Thanks to that historic traffic, Liverpool and Southampton remain inextricably twinned with New York. Make no mistake: though Cunard's fleet was built, registered and manned in Great Britain, the company's appeal no less than its major patronage has always been skewed unerringly towards America. Long before the English-Speaking Union was formally established in 1920, Samuel Cunard had laid the groundwork, forging geographical no less than emotional ties between Britons and Americans embarking aboard his company tonnage.

I must explain that, in the pages to follow, readers will find no more than passing reference to the company's heroic role throughout two world wars. The topic deserves a separate book and, more importantly, ocean liners' wartime deployment remains the very antithesis of progress. However noble Cunard's response to both contingencies, brave crewmen and -women died and dozens of ships were destroyed. For merchant fleets, war is a brutal *force majeur* that puts growth on hold.

Whence my durable fascination with ocean liners? I can think of at least three cogent reasons. First, my Scottish kinsman, Thomas Graham, later Lord Lynedoch, was the first passenger accommodated on the first steam-powered ocean liner. He embarked with his nephew, Robert Graham, aboard the American *Savannah* in Stockholm for passage to St. Petersburg in the fall of 1819.

Second, as the child of Scottish and American parents, it follows naturally that ocean crossings between Old World and New were rituals of my youth. Transatlantic travel became an addictive component of my life from the age of six months on.

Finally, I am reminded of a telling childhood experience at a Connecticut summer camp in August 1940. Two other boys and I were charged with delivering a huge cauldron of cocoa to an overnight camping site across the lake. We did so by rowboat, the steaming cocoa a simulacrum funnel amidships. As we rowed, I had with me a two-chime whistle with which we hooted our way through tendrils of nighttime mist. To impressionable eleven-years-olds—and a future maritime historian in particular—this was compelling ocean liner play, a haunting nocturnal voyage I have never forgotten and irreplaceable fodder for an author/lecturer who, today, spends half his fortuitous life at sea.

The North Atlantic can be a daunting maritime arena, guaranteeing hard-fought passage across the most forbidding ocean of the world's seven. Winter storms are acknowledged as appalling but, as any transatlantic captain will advise you, unpredictable weather can be encountered every month of the year.

Small wonder that these trackless, turbulent wastes remain, indubitably and reassuringly, Cunard country.

John Maxtone-Graham
February, 2004

The Major Cunarders from 1840 to 2004

BRITANNIA 1840-1848
1,135 grt. - 9 knots

PERSIA 1856-1867
3,300 grt.-13.5 knots

SERVIA 1881-1901
7,392 grt. - 16 knots

UMBRIA 1884-1910
7,718 grt. - 19 knots

CAMPANIA 1893-1914
12,950 grt. - 21 knots

CARMANIA 1905-1931
19,524 grt. - 18 knots

LUSITANIA 1907-1915
31,550 grt. - 25 knots

MAURETANIA (I) 1907-1934
31,938 grt. - 25 knots

AQUITANIA 1914-1949
45,647 grt. - 23 knots

BERENGARIA 1920-1938
52,226 grt. - 22 knots

QUEEN MARY 1936-1967
81,237 grt. - 29 knots

MAURETANIA (II) 1939-1965
35,738 grt. - 23 knots

QUEEN ELIZABETH 1946-1968
83,673 grt. - 29 knots

CARONIA 1949-1967
34,183 grt. - 22 knots

QUEEN ELIZABETH 2 1969-
70,327 grt. - 28.5 knots

QUEEN MARY 2 2004-
150,000 grt. - 29.3 knots

The Giant in Prospect

*Perhaps, with your knowledge of North Atlantic liners,
you should try and arrive at your own design; only then
can we assess whether it makes economic sense.*

—Carnival Chairman Micky Arison, in preliminary conversation
with his naval architect Stephen Payne

Queen Mary 2 rose like a great gray behemoth from the bottom of Alstom Chantiers de l'Atlantique's longest dry dock.

Sprawling Alstom Chantiers de l'Atlantique is the central industrial complex of the town of St.-Nazaire, situated where the Loire debouches into the Atlantic. There, for more than a century and a half, an evocative parade of French Line tonnage has been produced, immortals such as *Paris, Ile de France, Normandie,* and the third *France.*

In modern times, the yard launches fleets of modern-day cruise ships. Only five can be produced annually, a reflection of available dry dock space and the yard's steel-cutting capability. Suiting her stupefying dimensions, *Queen Mary 2* was assigned the logistical descriptive of "1.6 ships," another unique distinction for this gigantic Cunarder.

From the very outset, *Queen Mary 2* was destined to astonish. She is the longest, broadest, and tallest passenger vessel ever launched, with an unprecedented gross tonnage of 150,000 tons. Costing $800 million, she is also the most expensive. She can tear along at 30 knots in the glorious tradition of predecessor *Queens.* With an overall length of 1,132 feet (*345meters*), she comfortably surpasses *Norway-ex-France* by a hundred feet. Her 147-foot (*45-meter*) beam at the bridge betrays her as too wide for Panama's canal. *QM2*'s draft is 32 feet (10 meters), identical to that of current flagship *Queen Elizabeth 2* but less than the two original *Queens.* From boot topping to funnel top, she towers above the waterline 203 feet (62 meters) and passengers sailing in and out of New York on her upper decks commune eye-to-eye with Lady Liberty.

Not merely a new Cunarder, *QM2* is unquestionably the greatest Cunarder of all time. Moreover, *mirabile dictu,* she is imbued with the exacting specifications of an ocean liner. Liners used to make line voyages from Britain to America in all seasons, sailing year-round, the very antithesis of today's shipboard-for-fun. Whereas cruise ships dawdle around exotic itineraries, ocean liners thundered across the world's most formidable oceans on bruising schedule. The only other ocean liner extant is *Queen Elizabeth 2,* launched in 1967 and previously considered "the last Atlantic liner." Now Cunard duplicated and amplified those demanding criteria for *QM2*.

Ships do not just materialize. Their heritage evolves from prior company (or rival) tonnage and they come into being thanks to the dogged labor of thousands. In the vanguard is the visionary, who seeks out experts—architect, engineer, shipbuilder, designer, planner, sailor, and administrator—and sets them to work. Their accumulated wisdom, experience and toil are *Queen Mary 2*'s life force, infusing shape, character, grace, and mobility into thousands of tons of inert steel.

The visionary is unquestionably Micky Arison, Chairman of Carnival Corporation. He surveys the world from a tenth-floor office at Carnival's Miami headquarters. The chairman is assured and ebullient, his beaming face adorned with rimless spectacles and a sandy moustache and goatee. At fifty-four, he is blessed with both the inspiration and the means to make extraordinary things happen in the shipping world.

His late father Ted founded Carnival Cruises back in 1972 with Canadian Pacific's *Empress of Canada.* Arison *père* re-christened her *Mardi Gras,* and, three remarkable decades after her first Miami sailing, Arison *fils* oversees an incredible fleet of sixty-six vessels producing annual revenues approaching seven billion dollars. The vessels of Carnival Cruise Lines, Costa Cruises, Cunard Line, Holland America Line, P&O/Princess Cruises, Seabourn Cruises, and Windstar Cruises operate as members of a giant consortium headquartered in Carnival's Miami office.

It was Micky Arison's bold decision to buy the ailing British company in 1998, assuring an infusion of cash, practicality, and drive. As Captain Ron Warwick of *Queen Elizabeth 2* said: "We are all delighted to be owned once again by a shipping line rather than a hotel chain." In fact, Arison had dreamed of building a contemporary ocean liner long before his purchase, identifying Cunard as the perfect instrument of his ambition.

"We bought Cunard," Arison says flat out, "to create *Queen Mary 2,* not the other way around. . . .This was around the time of the *Titanic* movie. We were all talking about this overwhelming nostalgia movement in

Opposite: *Queen Mary 2* under construction in Forme B, the yard's largest dry dock. Note how the bulbous bow still sports the brackets essential to its assembly.

the country. What if we built the next great ocean liner?" The fabled White Star liner had contributed its potent mystique into the mix and set Arison on the road to acquisition and construction.

Of the dozens of newbuildings that he has ushered into service, none was more challenging. To implement his dream, exactly the right expert was in-house. The pivotal member of Carnival's newbuilding team is Stephen Payne, a brilliant young naval architect, a born and bred Londoner. He has been intimately involved with a succession of Carnival newbuildings since his initial employment by UK shipbuilding consultants TMP (Technical Marine Planning) in 1985. Payne was involved with designing Carnival's *Holiday* and, later, the company's *Fantasy*, delivered in 1990.

It was an episode from the television program *Blue Peter* that first fired seven-year-old Payne's imagination. Footage from a *Queen Elizabeth* 1967 Channel crossing conveyed the majesty of the great Cunarder and he was hooked. A horrific 1972 *Blue Peter* broadcast captured live images of his beloved *Queen Elizabeth* afire in Hong Kong harbor. In the program's *Blue Peter Annual*, a writer hazarded that a comparable liner would never be built. Payne recalls, "I wrote to the program to say that I thought they were wrong and that one day there might be. I still have their reply, wishing me well and hoping that such a vision might some day come true. Well, the rest is history!"

Physically, Payne is an Englishman's Englishman, of medium height with a beaming, almost Dickensian visage. A top-ranked schoolboy-debater, Payne is a formidable speaker, devastatingly well informed. His platform style is meticulous but never dull, the words delivered with a pungent South London accent.

Second *Queen Mary*'s inception was unconventional. Traditionally, when asked to design a newbuilding, a naval architect asks three essential questions: How many passengers? How fast? How luxurious? But for

this assignment, the chairman was obliged to reverse the order of things. Before specifying capacity, speed, or lavishness, he needed informed guidance. So naval architect Payne ultimately defined for owner Arison the exacting maritime parameters he sought.

Payne was instructed to embark on an extensive study as to what form a viable and economically sound twenty-first century ocean liner should take. Arison concluded his brief: "Stephen, in your lifetime, you will only have one opportunity to design such a ship so you had better get it right the first time!" Moments later, he added: "After this ship, I don't quite know what I am going to give you to follow on. Nothing will ever compare with this." Payne had been entrusted with contemporary shipbuilding's dream commission: Project *Queen Mary* was under way.

He and colleague Richard Moore began their two-year study in May 1998. One inescapable mantra guided Payne: "You cannot place a ship in regular North Atlantic service in the near winter months unless you have a true liner." He is haunted by the ordeal of the Italian Line's *Michelangelo* as she was being driven through a storm to New York in April 1966. A monster wave engulfed the bow, killing two passengers and a crewman. Payne was determined that his *Queen Mary 2* would incorporate epic invulnerability.

Every liner shares several essential characteristics: high speed, buttoned-up superstructure, a long bow deck, engines amidships, lifeboats high above the waterline, deep draft, and a finely shaped hull. Few if any contemporary newbuildings meet those relentless criteria. Standard cruising speed seldom exceeds 20 knots, tall top hampers are crowded forward, draft is restricted for in-port maneuvering, and, between finely wrought bow and stern, hulls are consistently flat. Since today's ships are assembled from prefabricated sections or blocks, keeping most of those giant Lego pieces rectangular makes economic sense.

Admittedly, a few cruise ships share some ocean liner proclivities. For sixth *Rotterdam*, Payne modified *Statendam*'s basic hull shape into something approaching a liner. He added length to derive an economical turn of speed and made the hull less boxy. By so doing, he sacrificed some stability but made it up by increasing her beam. But those refinements did not make *Rotterdam*

a real liner. No legitimate ocean liner had been built since *QE2* of 1969. Faced with the task of designing one three decades later, Payne was fully aware that shipbuilding has changed radically; moreover, today's passenger expectations have change as well.

Something similar to *QE2* was the obvious answer. But whereas St.-Nazaire categorized *QM2* as "1.6 of a ship," she would also represent 1.4 of a ship in financial terms. The power required to drive the vessel at speed; the increased thickness, strength, and weight of structural components; and the potential loss of revenue within a shaped rather than boxy hull had to be factored in.

One of his earliest tasks was to analyze *QE2*'s thirty-year track record. Payne was very familiar with her interior design. He finds her staircase system "immensely confusing," an inevitable outcome of early building decisions. Originally designed for three classes, *QE2* entered service hastily modified for two; nowadays, her passengers are accommodated essentially within a single class. The "promenade deck" is really incorporated within the Queens Room and passengers tramping around the Boat Deck cannot easily complete a circuit because of high winds.

QE2's top five decks are fabricated of aluminum. An enormous plus for stability, it allowed inclusion of one more deck than if her superstructure were steel alone. Nevertheless, aluminum involves some disadvantages. Though one-sixth the weight of steel, it is less dense and it hardens with age, changing characteristics. These days, *QE2*'s superstructure has lost much of its initial resiliency.

Payne decided early on that *QM2* should be all steel, a resolve that carried potent ramifications in the matter of size. By substituting five steel for aluminum decks, it was clear that he would end up with a ship smaller than *QE2*, because stability requirements meant that he would be obliged to have one less deck. But conversely, the project's economics demanded that *QM2* not be smaller than *QE2* but bigger. Indeed, the inevitability of that mammoth expansion was guaranteed as Arison added marketing demands into the technological mix; no sooner had one set of amendments been incorporated and re-submitted than further increases were requested. Like Alice in Wonderland,

Queen Mary 2 "just grew and grew," assuming her present, record-breaking dimensions.

In fact, the only limitations to a ship's size are twofold: Her length must allow sufficient maneuvering room within both homeport and ports of call and she must pass beneath every bridge spanning every itinerary. *QM2*'s overall length of 1,136 feet (346 meters) creates no problem in Southampton; the Queen Elizabeth II terminal encompasses her length without difficulty. Arriving off the terminal, *QM2* executes a complete 180-degree turn before docking portside to, bows pointing down-harbor. There is a more than adequate radius of 1500 feet (457 meters) between the berth and a limiting channel marker identified as the Hythe Knock.

In New York harbor, length is not a problem either, although 34 feet (10-plus meters) of second *Queen Mary*'s hull jut out beyond the end of the 1100-foot (335-meter) North River Passenger Ship Terminal piers. Similarly, there is sufficient room for her to back out and turn down-river for departure. Indeed, New York's only prohibitive limitation is height. *Queen Mary 2*'s formidable 203-foot (62-meter) air draft is the maximum permissible. Payne had to restrict the elevation of both mast and funnel top in order to leave ten feet (three-plus meters) of clearance below the roadway of the Verrazzano Narrows Bridge. As he jests ruefully, "If we haven't got it right, it will only be a problem the first time; either the bridge or the funnel will disappear."

Next, Payne had to submit his hull to the demands it would encounter in service, within a model-testing tank. Carnival's chosen facility was MARIN (Maritime Research Institute). Europe's largest deep water and offshore testing facility, it is located in the Netherlands town of Wageningen. Over much of the year 2000, two yellow models of the *Queen Mary 2* hull—one large and one smaller—were built and tested at MARIN. Both betrayed the brute strength and pronounced flare of the real ship's bows, reminiscent of both *Queen*

Above, left: Queen Mary 2's inspired naval architect Stephen Payne. Above, right: Inverted bottom sections for Queen Mary 2 take shape in one of the yard's steel assembly sheds. Opposite: Dwarfed by engine-room machinery, a welder plies his dazzling trade.

Elizabeth 2 and original *Queen Mary*. But because of the hull's three decks of cabin balconies, Payne had amplified the bow's protective flare to divert oncoming waves more efficiently to either side.

In turn, each model was launched into MARIN's largest tank, an indoor cement trough nearly 600 feet (180 meters) long, 131 feet (40 meters) wide and 16 feet (5 meters) deep. First towed to determine resistance, then subsequently self-propelled to ascertain powering requirements, the model's form was continually refined to improve performance. For subsequent sea-keeping tests, the smaller of the two models was employed, linked to the carriage by a multi-conductor umbilical cord. Equipped with both propellers and stabilizers, this smaller model could be propelled and steered from "shore" by radio command.

The tank's water can be roiled to produce anything from minor turbulence to fearsome rollers. For days, as computers monitored her performance, *QM2's* hull was run at varying speeds through a gauntlet of increasingly ominous sea conditions. The bow configuration proved admirable. Persevering at 20 knots through "hurricane-sized" waves, potential inundations were shrugged efficiently aside.

Next, MARIN wanted to analyze the stern's performance. The smaller *QM2* model was liberated from the towing bridle and waves were generated to impact the after end. Payne's final design combined a modified transom with elements of first *Queen Mary's* cruiser

Opposite: Stephen Payne determined that the solution for the vessel's after end is the "Constanzi" stern, combining both cruiser and transom sterns. What's in a bow? *Above*: QE2 in midocean and model QM2 in a tank negotiate testing waves.

stern; described as the "Constanzi stern," a similar arrangement had been pioneered for *Oceanic* and *Eugenio C* in the mid-1960s. The hybrid was necessary because a simple transom stern, slapped by a following sea, can set up troublesome vibrations. But the *Queen Mary 2* version had to be further refined to provide appropriate "landing spaces" for her propellers.

The model's four working stabilizers were located as on the full-scale prototype—two a side amidships. Payne was anxious to know not only how they would damp rolling but also what corrective effect they exerted with a following sea. Subjected to a wave onslaught from astern, model *QM2* exhibited a hunting instinct; the hull cycled through random, sideslipping undulations. When waves were amplified, the movement became so pronounced that propellers tended to draw air from the surface down into their wash. But remedial application of the stabilizers minimized the hunting instinct and vastly improved *QM2's* longitudinal stability.

This is obviously the moment to describe *Queen Mary 2's* remarkable propulsion system. She is the first quadruple-screwed vessel to appear on the North Atlantic since *France* of 1962. But apart from their number, everything else about *QM2's* propeller quartet is radically different. Each one is mounted on a separate pod suspended beneath the hull. Though the two forward pods are fixed, the after two can turn through 360 degrees, obviating the need for a rudder. *QM2* is steered instead by her two azimuthing, or rotating, pods. The electrical power required to drive the vessel's propellers comes from four diesel generators below and two 25-kilowatt gas turbines beneath the funnel, each chambered within a soundproof enclosure.

Payne's hull passed her MARIN tests with flying colors.

Now we should document his upper deck choices. Some ocean liner aficionados had hoped that *Queen Mary 2* might be topped with three stacks. But Payne never even considered it, pointing out that every ton of top weight demands a two-ton compensation below decks. Moreover, Payne was determined that nothing should sully his profile. That said, he did succumb to some minor upper deck fakery, an ingenious *trompe l'oeil* device adorning the corners of his bridge screen, in effect the vessel's windshield. By application of two decks' worth of painted, wrap-around black lines, Payne has visually recapitulated original *Queen Mary*'s forward deck crossovers.

Structurally, the second *Queen Mary*'s bridge screen radiates strength and reliability. Vastly compelling is its complexity of curves, a traditional bowed front (first *Queen Mary* again) that slopes as well, cone-shaped, rising to the formidable brow of the bridge and doubly convex for strength. Perhaps most distinctive are its stout corners, gracefully sloping brackets that tie all superstructure decks together while incorporating yet another audacious curve—concave, this time—into the mix of planes. Would that poor *Michelangelo* had boasted such an enviable forward rampart!

Amidships, *QM2*'s overriding profile feature is her towering, single funnel, rendering homage to the continuum of predecessor flagship. But there is not a shred of *QE2* continuum the length of *QM2*'s flanks. Superstructure and hull are perforated with rows of balconies. Their presence *in extenso* cogently underscores how much shipboard has changed since *QE2*'s 1969 debut. Not one cabin balcony had been incorporated into her original design, although random balconied suites were subsequently stacked atop her upper decks. But by way of contrast, eight *QM2* decks are festooned with balconies. The bottom three balcony rows are inset (uniquely) within the hull. Fully three-quarters of *Queen Mary 2*'s cabins come complete with open-air terraces.

With hull and general arrangement completed and approved, the next step was for shipyards to submit construction tenders on June 4, 1999. Kiel's HDW yard bowed out; the project was just too big. Similarly, the excellent German yard at Pappenberg was disqualified by limitations of their building shed. Finland's MASA yard's interest was forbade by preordained building schedules; their capacious Turku dry docks had been preempted by Royal Caribbean International's *Voyager*-class newbuildings. Similarly, Italy's Monfalcone order book was full of Princess and Carnival Destiny tonnage. Closer to home, the venerable Belfast yard of Harland & Wolff had internal financing limitations that could not accommodate the scale of the *QM2* undertaking.

The French won out. A letter of intent with Alstom Chantiers de l'Atlantique at St.-Nazaire was signed in

March of 2000, and in November, a final building contract certified delivery for December 2003. Here was a double first—first Cunarder built in a French yard and first *Queen* constructed outside the United Kingdom.

This moment conjures up the opening vision of this chapter. The vessel's optimum shape had been determined, and its steel shell perfected. Stephen Payne is proud of its groundbreaking qualifications. "*Queen Mary 2* is probably the strongest and most adequately designed transatlantic liner to date." Although liners traditionally anticipated a three-decade life expectancy, Payne posited "a forty-year fatigue life" for *QM2*.

The next step was for Cunard and its appointed interior designers to decorate and furnish their giant steel structure. Having examined *QM2*'s exterior, it is time to meet Cunard's management and their chosen designers before embarking into the belly of the beast.

Above: One of the *QM2*'s four amazing Mermaid pods is moved into position. The vessel's remarkable propulsion system includes two fixed forward pods and two rear pods that rotate 360 degrees. *Opposite*: Second *Queen Mary* floated quietly off the dry dock floor. *Overleaf*: Invited travel press representatives pose in a grandstand beneath *Queen Mary 2*'s completed bow in March 2003.

CHANTIERS DE L'ATLANTIQUE

Opposite: The bulbous bow complete, bow sections above it are still open to the skies. *Above:* Down these emerging twin staircases over the years to come, thousands of *QM2* passengers will descend to dine.

Above: A haunting view of G32 juxtaposed against St.-Nazaire's suspension bridge spanning the Loire. *Opposite*: A pair of welders work intently within segregated steel compartments of an overturned bottom section.

Cunard Enrichment

When you first you come on board, if you half-close your eyes,
you will sense immediately that you are on a liner from the
twenties or thirties. But open them fully and you will realize
at once that the décor is also strikingly contemporary.

—Fredrik Johanssen, Tillberg Design

Only when every square inch of *Queen Mary 2's* dimensions had been approved could Payne hand over the final "block form" GA (general arrangement) to those charged with cladding and finishing her interiors and deckscapes.

That work began in April 1999. Through the auspices of their selected designers, the character and décor of every cabin, public room, staircase, deck, and alleyway would be established. It was a lengthy and complex process, as demanding as Payne's initial design chores. Three and a half years' worth of logistical, practical, and aesthetic choices had to be made: a continuous selecting, winnowing, and approval process that extended right up to delivery day in December 2003.

Cunard's head office had been relocated from its traditional Manhattan venue south to Florida in 1997, a year before the company was acquired by Carnival. Today, Cunard occupies several floors of a verdantly landscaped office tower along Blue Lagoon Drive, hard by Miami Airport. Leading the Cunard Line is Pamela Conover, a Carnival alumna who was appointed COO in 1998 and president in 2001.

Any overview of Conover's life reveals two dominant threads, a career fabric woven inextricably with financial warp and maritime woof. After working as a teller at the London office of Wells Fargo Bank, Conover requested a transfer to Wells Fargo's New York office where she studied to become a credit analyst. Her maiden venture into the shipping world was as assistant treasurer for the container shipping company United States Lines.

In the mid-1980s, Pam Conover moved on to Citicorp, appointed Vice-President of the ship financing department. In 1992, she was promoted to managing director of the company's entire North American ship financing business. Not surprisingly, one of Citicorp's foremost clients was the Carnival Corporation.

Two years later, when Carnival invested in Epirotiki Cruise Lines, Pam Conover was selected to become President and CEO of the eastern Mediterranean carrier. And when Carnival divested itself of Epirotiki in 1995, Conover was invited to come aboard at Carnival, assigned the post of Vice-President for Strategic Planning. It was that position that served as springboard for her Cunard posting, first as Chief Operating Officer under former President Larry Pimentel, then assumption of his position following his resignation.

Conover's right hand at Cunard is Deborah Natansohn, who holds the pivotal position of Senior Vice-President for Sales and Marketing. Over the course of her career, New Yorker Natansohn has profited from a wealth of in-depth travel and cruise experience. After graduating from State University of New York, Albany in 1974, Natansohn took a post with *Trade Travel* magazine before moving on for a five-year stint as Director of Marketing for Travelers International, where her clients included TWA Getaway, SAS Viking Vacations, and, significantly, Cunard Europe. Subsequently, Natansohn was immersed within the hands-on administration of various cruise lines, serving as Vice-President for Marketing at both Ocean Lines and Pearl Cruises and later, as Senior Vice-President for Orient Lines. Natansohn served in that capacity for six years before assuming the presidency in 1998. In 2000, when Orient was sold to Norwegian Cruise Line, she was invited by Larry Pimentel and Pam Conover to join Cunard in her present capacity. Cunard's two top-ranked executives make an ideal team, Conover's financial expertise dovetailing perfectly with Natansohn's marketing and sales strengths. "This was a company," muses Pam Conover "with fantastic brand equity." Restoring and burnishing that brand is their top priority.

In addition to port and starboard, every passenger vessel has two additional sides, the hotel and marine departments. Aboard *Queen Mary 2*, the hotel side is under the capable direction of Vice-President for Hotel Operations Lawrence Rapp. Thirty-eight years ago, Larry started with Matson Line, followed by stints with American Hawaii and Pearl Cruises and Royal Viking Line. He was subsequently instrumental in the start-up of Seabourn Cruises. Larry oversees all *QM2* hotel matters, including furnishings, food, drink, cabins, and entertainment.

Opposite: Graceful, curving twin staircases join Decks 2 and 3 in *QM2's* Grand Lobby. (© Michel Verdure)

His opposite number on the technical side, supervising all of *Queen Mary 2*'s formidable maritime requirements, is Milton Gonzales, Cunard's Vice-President of Marine & Technical Operations. A graduate of Duke University and the U.S. Merchant Marine Academy, Gonzales worked for fourteen years as director of Sea-Land Containers before coming aboard at Cunard. His present responsibilities include every detail of *QM2*'s marine and technical specifics, a cornucopia that includes safety, security, and port operations.

Third member of the company's senior triumvirate is Vice-President for Business Development Edie Bornstein, dauntingly articulate, enthusiastic, and persuasive, master of the cold call. She has marshaled an exemplary collection of cultural institutions, chefs, and retailers into the tenor of *QM2* shipboard, prestigious components from both sides of the Atlantic.

She was instrumental, for example, in bringing vintner Veuve-Clicquot onboard, assigning its name permanently to the Champagne Bar and, significantly, to the bottle that christened the vessel. She also signed on two celebrated American chefs. Daniel Boulud—*wunderkind* of Manhattan's superb Daniel's Restaurant—was recruited as culinary adviser for the vessel's menus in the main restaurant. Prolific restaurateur Todd English was invited to set

up his own shipboard restaurant on board. Bornstein followed up on Deborah Natansohn's brainstorm for RADA—London's famous Royal Academy of Dramatic Art—to create a shipboard theatrical repertory company. Thanks to Bornstein, Chanel, Dunhill, Burberry, and Harrods each have a specialty shop on board. Likewise, Bornstein implemented Enrichment Director Mary Thomas's inspiration that visiting academics from Oxford University's Continuing Education Department should embark as a core ConneXions faculty, ensuring peerless academic input for passengers. Veuve-Clicquot, Daniel Boulud, Todd English, RADA, Oxford, Chanel, Dunhill— the names speak for themselves.

With his naval architect's exterior a given, Micky Arison had next to assign the task of creating the vessel's interiors. His final decision was to divide the commission between two design entities: Sweden's Tillberg Design would be responsible for 80 percent of *QM2* while designteam, a younger London firm, would handle the remainder.

Robert Tillberg was a designer new to Arison until a recently completed *QE2* renovation. Pre-eminent in his field, Tillberg is a tall, ruddy Swede with an enviable, forty-year maritime track record encompassing more than sixty passenger vessels. Today, Robert Tillberg is perfectly attuned to the kind of upscale, distinguished finish that owners demand, his public rooms exhibiting what a contemporary journalist has described as "luxuriant functionalism."

Tillberg Design boasts a worldwide presence. The head office is in Viken, a Swedish village near Helsingborg. The original structure has grown into a complex of generously windowed buildings, awash with light and free-flowing interiors. Members of his design team work together in a new addition offering an offshore view of the Öresund, through which vessels they have designed periodically sail. These days, Tillberg lives in La Baule, convenient to nearby St.-Nazaire. Yet however remote from his native Sweden, throughout

Above: Some of Cunard's top executives: seated, Pamela Conover and, left to right, Christine Steinberg, Debbie Natansohn, Edie Bornstein, and Helen Panagos. *Opposite:* A sample of Cunard's haute couture teaser ads, featuring models dreaming about *Queen Mary 2*.

Can you wait?

QM2

his *oeuvre*, one detects haunting reminders of Viken's tranquil, mid-summer, northern light.

His son Tomas heads up the firm's Fort Lauderdale branch. A convenient adjacency of that office to Carnival and Cunard in Miami ensured first-hand participation throughout the tentative initial design phase. Both Tillbergs, father and son, collaborated closely with Stephen Payne on the shape of the new Cunarder's provocative forward profile.

Tillberg's London headquarters is an English design firm called SMC. There, Andy Collier—a senior partner and "C" of the firm's triple-initial name—has been appointed Project Leader of the entire *Queen Mary 2* undertaking. Tillberg's designated man for *Queen Mary 2* is Fredrik Johansson, a tall, genial Swede.

The other design firm hired for *QM2* was designteam, a successful company established only five years ago in London by partners Eric Mouzourides and Frank Symeou. They have been designated lead designers for *Queen Victoria,* Cunard's latest newbuilding in Italy. The partners strive to combine a high degree of professionalism—read solid experience—with innovative freshness.

Designteam's areas of responsibility aboard *Queen Mary 2* include Illuminations, its surrounding Cunard Academy, Todd English's restaurant on Deck 8, as well as all Grand Lobby's shops on Deck 3. The balance of the interiors were created by Tillberg Design, including the Grand Lobby, Royal Court Theatre, Britannia Restaurant, Queens and Princess Grills, Commodore Club, the Queens Room, Canyon Ranch SpaClub, and all cabins and staircases.

A Dutch company called Art & Enterprise was contracted to provide all of *QM2*'s works of art, a substantial collection valued at $5,000,000. From among their international stable of artists, Art & Enterprise has commissioned sculpture, bas-reliefs, tapestry, paintings, and prints.

Devised by a London company called the Open Agency is Maritime Quest, an in-depth, visual retrospective of Cunard history. Informative wall panels containing text, photographs, paintings, and drawings document the company's transatlantic past. Passengers can enjoy the entire series merely *en passant* or in more studious depth via a hand-held, audio-guide device available at the Purser's desk.

Now that we have met Cunard's brass and introduced the designers, it is time to explore the vessel itself. In total, *Queen Mary 2* has seventeen decks stacked one atop another. Two of them are ghost decks, because they do not exist as identifiable entities (read on). And the lowest four—double bottom, Deck B, Deck A, and Deck 1—do not, save with one exception, involve passengers.

The double bottom houses much of the ship's machinery. The vessel's crew are housed the length of Deck A and the forward part of Deck 1 just above it. They must descend one level for off-duty entertainment, to Deck B's pub, cinema, and gymnasium. Conversely, the crew ascends from their living quarters for meals, for the crew galley lies along Deck 1's port side amidships. Nearby are separate crew, staff, and officers' messes. There is another Pub—Cunard crews' traditional Pig & Whistle—on the same deck.

Passengers tendering ashore when *Queen Mary 2* is anchored out will descend to one of Deck 1's four tender embarkation lounges, named Kensington, Belgravia, Knightsbridge, and Chelsea. Throughout sea days, these same passenger-friendly spaces will serve a multiplicity of uses. One, for example, becomes a card room, and aerobic classes dominate another. Belgravia can double as supplementary waiting room for the ship's hospital while Kensington will accommodate overflow of large cocktail parties held in the adjacent officers' wardroom.

Given that Deck 1 is the supportive cellar of the main galley directly above it, nearly all its after end is devoted to provision and preparation rooms. Throughout this lower-deck warren, consignments of meat, poultry, fish, and produce are retrieved from cold storage. We will discover, as we progress upward through *QM2*'s hull, that nearly all the ship's galleys are situated on a vertical path rising above this deck's preparation complex.

Above: Robert Tillberg pauses on one of the vessel's staircases, pleased with the successful completion of one of his most challenging commissions. *Opposite:* The Queens Room aboard *Queen Mary 2* continues the *QE2* tradition—an exhilarating space for dancing and occasional cabaret. (© MICHEL VERDURE)

One level higher, on Deck 2 amidships, *QM2* backstage metamorphoses dramatically into fore stage, where the deadly serious business of *Queen Mary 2* begins. No more crucial shipboard venue exists than a liner's threshold. Harried, flight-weary passengers, laden with hand luggage and sprung from the ennui of pierside check-in, troop aboard their vessel, a moment anticipated for months.

What do they find? They are welcomed into the Grand Lobby, a towering atrium, enriched with panoramic glass elevators floating upward through six decks. Ranged along Grand Lobby's starboard side is the Purser's Desk, fount of welcome and problem solving. Across the forward wall, shore excursion desks await. Visible along the Grand Lobby's port side is the Empire Casino. The complimentary space to starboard is occupied by the cozy snuggery of Cunard's signature Golden Lion Pub.

Incorporated between Decks 2 and 3 is unseen but pivotal Deck 3L, the first of the two "ghost decks" mentioned earlier. This subtle, naval architectural legerdemain augments Deck 2's verticality, imparting monumental grandeur to its major public rooms. In fact, Decks 2, 3L, and 3 are united within one overwhelming cathedral of height for much of their length.

From the Grand Lobby, we can turn left to go aft or right to go forward. Let us proceed left into the Britannia Restaurant. The scale is sumptuous, the dimensions breath-taking. Accommodating over thirteen hundred passengers at a sitting, the restaurant is composed of two, hull-wide levels, the lower one on Deck 2 amplified by a commodious balcony level up on 3. Payne has rewarded us with the first Cunarder since *Berengaria* to offer a double-tiered dining room.

Proceed with me across an after staircase lobby into the Queen's Room, venue for music, dancing, and occasional cabaret. Unlike any other of the Decks 2 and 3 public rooms, the Queens Room boasts only one level, sited as it is atop the galley. Regardless, the space is impressive, incorporating a large, recessed ceiling. The bandstand is sited along the room's after wall, framed

prettily within an art deco, half-round proscenium. In addition to offering nightly dancing and cabaret, the Queens Room is where passengers will each be photographed shaking hands with the captain.

Conversely, if we exit forward from Britannia Restaurant's upper level, we meander towards the bow en route to shows just the other side of the Grand Lobby. Deck 3's level surrounding the Grand Lobby is bar country. To starboard we pass the Chart Room. Hard by it is the Veuve-Clicquot Champagne Bar, to port Sir Samuel's Wine Bar. The remaining quadrants around the Grand Lobby on Deck 3 are given over to the Mayfair Shops where clothing, souvenirs, jewelry, perfume, books, and sundries are on inviting display.

Directly forward is the first of *Queen Mary*'s two great entertainment facilities, one sited directly beyond the other. The Royal Court Theatre, named after London's original, is an ambitiously well-equipped show lounge, accommodating an audience of just over eleven hundred. Incorporated within it is an arsenal of sophisticated stage machinery the Sloane Square original might well envy. Within its proscenium arch, the stage not only revolves, but is also divided into four athwartship platforms, each one of which can be elevated by remote command to varying heights. Another roving platform is situated at the bottom of the orchestra pit. If required, a show band playing in the pit can rise magically on cue to orchestra floor level before proceeding upstage as far as the back wall, a stunning scenic effect. A capacious fly floor stores flats and fiber optical drops out of sight and a stage-wide video wall that can be flown in and out on demand.

Situated immediately beyond the Royal Court Theatre is another, smaller amphitheater christened Illuminations. Designteam's triple-threat space fulfills several multi-media roles as cinema, lecture hall, and, incredibly, a working planetarium. Far out at sea, Illuminations can conjure up peerless celestial displays fully the equal of those mounted within shore-side planetaria.

Within a state-of-the-art projection booth, twin 35-millimeter projectors guarantee a contemporary shipboard rarity: superb film screenings. Already a unique plus aboard *Queen Elizabeth 2*, in these days of inferior videotaped movies shown elsewhere, first-class

Opposite: Overlooking the atrium, the Veuve-Clicquot Champagne Bar is a place to sample several vintages while nibbling on fine caviar. (© MICHEL VERDURE)

theatrical projection continues gloriously aboard *Queen Mary 2*.

The close contiguity of these two auditoria, one located directly ahead of the other, necessitated some last-minute GA refinement. Micky Arison asked Joe Farcus, his resident interior architect, how best to achieve either one of *QM2*'s performance venues without neglecting the other and without confusing passengers.

A man with fine-tuned antennae about assisting passengers through complex deck schemes, Joe recommended shrinking the Royal Court's lateral dimension sufficiently to permit provision of flanking promenades. Readily accessible and identifiable from the Royal Court Theatre's lobby, these vital detours invite those bound for movie rather than show to bypass Royal Court and continue forward to Illuminations.

En route, they will find yet a third entertainment option, another *QM2* novelty. Anticipating the lobby of Illuminations is ConneXions, a spread of seven sizable "class rooms" devoted to interactive passenger instruction, dubbed the Cunard Academy. Within this floating academia, expandable spaces offer specialized talks and seminars to passenger participants on a wide variety of subjects.

Farcus must be given credit for Grand Lobby's towering atrium. During the original design phase, Cunard President Larry Pimentel had felt that an atrium was unnecessary. But the Arison/Farcus consensus was that passengers would expect one. Aft of that now Grand(er) Lobby, the challenge of bypassing Royal Court to achieve Illuminations is repeated towards the stern where Britannia Restaurant interfaces with Queen's Room. Joe recommended creation of what he describes as "mini-atriums" to facilitate entry into the Queens Room along both Decks 2 and 3. And once more, thanks to "ghost" Deck L3, two flanking promenades—the same kind that access Illuminations—circumvent Britannia's lower level.

Final destination, thanks to Deck 3L, is the vessel's diminutive, late-night hideaway, the G32 Room, named after this fourth *Queen*'s St.-Nazaire hull number and reminiscent of the Q4 Club on *QE2*'s original deck plan. Since it is a completely interior space, every afternoon teenagers will gather either for dancing or every adolescent's inevitable preference, hanging out.

Our horizontal walkabout throughout Decks 2, 3L, and 3 concluded, let us ascend. The next three levels up—Decks 4, 5, and 6—are devoted almost exclusively to passenger cabins. The sole exception is a complex for *Queen Mary 2*'s younger set located on the after end of Deck 6. Indoors, children of all ages are welcomed into either a nursery staffed by trained nannies or playrooms full of games, toys and all those electronic gadgets that often only young minds and hands can master. Outdoors, looking over the stern, is a children's swimming area, with a small splash pool forward and, though a larger body of water, what deck plans still describe as the "minnows" pool.

We emerge on Deck 7 (topmost stop for Grand Lobby's panoramic elevators) to encounter the vessel's third great public room deck. This level of *Queen Mary 2* also incorporates the second of Stephen Payne's "ghost decks," identified on his plan simply as Open 'Tween Deck. Were Deck 7 to be assigned a generic name, it would surely be Promenade Deck, as an inviting quarter-mile of teak enwraps the entire deckhouse.

After one exploratory circumnavigation, let us retrace our steps to explore Deck 7's forward interior. Immediately, we are engulfed within an epicurean complex dedicated to a paradoxical combination of

Above: A glorious expanse of celestial geography appears as if by magic within the finished dome. *Opposite:* Illumination's planetarium dome is rigged for viewing, shown here lowered from its stored position within the ceiling.

self-improvement and self-indulgence. Canyon Ranch SpaClub is *Queen Mary 2*'s state-of-the-art wellness center. It is a lavish facility that promotes therapy rather than mere products. Gymnasium and weight rooms share the view over the bow and, just aft, within two dozen treatment rooms, experienced Canyon Ranch personnel offer a healthful and rejuvenating cornucopia—massages and body work, mud, aromatherapy, ayuvedic and seaweed treatments, facials and masks, wraps and body scrubs. There is a central pool, and in the adjacent Thermal Suite, aromatic steam room and Finnish sauna.

Just aft is the Winter Garden. This wicker-furnished retreat is a perfect venue for tea. It is also a space for a quiet read, a companionable chat, knitting and needlepoint, a game of patience or post-prandial dozing. Gastronomy reigns the balance of Deck 7. We enter first into Kings Court, the vessel's lido, to use the generic term. Suiting *QM2*'s transatlantic stance, it has no outdoor tables but, to either side, five windowed bays compensate nicely by extending the interior out into flanking promenades. However, it does contain several intriguing catering alternatives. At dusk, Kings Court is transformed into four contrasting restaurants. Reserving tables through a central reservation number, passengers can dine in either the oriental Lotus, the British Carvery, *trattoria* La Piazza or, perhaps most intriguing, the innovative Chef's Galley. In the latter, thirty-five lucky diners will watch that evening's dinner-to-come being prepared, gratifying passengers' insatiable curiosity about shipboard food, its consumption no less than its preparation.

Opposite: Exclusive shipboard headquarters for pampered indolence, the thalassotherapy pool of the Canyon Ranch Spa Club. (© MICHEL VERDURE) *Above:* A view of the Winter Garden's wicker furniture with Ian Cairnie's palm-foliated conservatory ceiling above it. (© MICHEL VERDURE)

At the after end of Deck 7 are two more dining rooms, re-appearances of familiar, upscale *QE2* originals, Queens Grill to starboard—complete with its own designated cocktail lounge—and Princess Grill to port, each with superb ocean views across the surrounding promenade. Here occupants of the ship's most expensive accommodations will breakfast, lunch, and dine at extended-hour sittings. Meals for both grills are prepared within a single, dedicated galley.

Up a level, overlooking a swimming terrace spanning the after end of Deck 8, is another restaurant, given the name of the American chef whose culinary inspiration defines it, Todd English. Diners will face aft through an athwartship span of glass, an identical venue to first *Queen Mary*'s fondly recalled Veranda Grill.

Directly above Todd English's establishment, Decks 9 and 10 are devoted exclusively to suites and cabins. But adorning Deck 11's after end is a private outdoor aerie for the exclusive use of Queens Grill passengers, the only class-restricted deck on board, complete with its own hot tub and bar.

Two decks higher, passengers once more emerge outdoors into the vessel's upper deck sports complex, a breath-taking two hundred feet (sixty one meters) above the sea. At the stern are dog kennels and the Boardwalk Café, haven for the fast food lunches that swimmers in damp bathing suits crave. Just forward of the funnel's embrace is a swimming pool, protected when necessary by a retractable glass roof. Forward of that is a vast open sun-bowl with another pool, surrounded by golf driving simulators, paddle and table tennis courts, and an indoor sports center and the Lookout.

Last on our inspection tour are the vessel's forward-facing interiors. By descending to Deck 7 and proceeding forward to the Canyon Ranch SpaClub, we

can re-ascend via one of the exterior panoramic eleva-tors tucked behind the bridge. Their vertical itinerary begins on Deck 7 and either one will carry us up to every public (and private) room sited within the bridge screen's generous arc.

But before we embark in our delightfully scenic conveyance, a lightning primer about the ship's geogra-phy. Dual coordinates—horizontal decks and vertical stairwells—are mandatory aboard every passenger ves-sel. *Queen Mary 2* has four staircases spread the length of the vessel, lettered A, B, C, and D from bow to stern. Although only three elevator cars serve less-used A and D, six respond to more heavily-trafficked B and C stair-cases near the vessel's center.

Now, slip into the starboard side's panoramic eleva-tor. Pushing the button for Deck 8, we are lofted upward one level to emerge into the ship's combined library and writing room. Connected directly aft is Ocean Books, duplication of that popular library /bookshop aboard *QE2*. On the port side is the beauty salon, a vertical extension of Canyon Ranch SpaClub, achieved from Deck 7 either by interior staircase or the portside's panoramic elevator.

One level higher, we enter within the great span of glass enclosing the Commodore Club, the only for-ward interior save the wheelhouse encompassing the entire bridge screen. This is an absolute must for cock-tails or entry into port. Ancillary space aft includes the Board Room to port for private meetings and, on the starboard side, the Cigar Lounge, a cozy retreat for Havana connoisseurs.

We resume our vertical tour to find that since Deck

10 is VIP country only, stopping there requires a special passkey. The bridge screen glass has been segmented again, offering forward views for four huge staterooms, each boasting an expanse of unparalleled *luxe*. The star-board side's Queen Elizabeth suite has as its mirrored equivalent to port, the Queen Mary suite. The two cen-tral accommodations—Queen Anne port of the keel line and Queen Victoria starboard—are achieved via the A Staircase.

After tiptoeing out, we rise to Deck 11, the end of this elevator line. Here we can enjoy a splendid open observation deck, enclosing at its center an interior space for meetings, perfectly named the Atlantic Room.

Had we been able to float upward one more level, we should have reached the bridge. Unlike many con-temporary cruise ships, no passenger lounge is sited above it. Former-president Pimentel had suggested to Payne that he incorporate such a feature, but tradi-tionalist Payne demurred. No Cunarder has ever had a public room atop the bridge and he was not anxious to create a precedent aboard *QM2*.

Arrival at the bridge serves as apropos moment to introduce the master. Captain Ron Warwick has been a familiar host to many *QE2* passengers; what better cap-stone to his career than continuing that role aboard the company's latest flagship?

Above: Behind the generous sweep of the bar in the Commodore Club, Henk Brandwijk's superb model of *QM2* is encased in glass. (© Michael Verdure) *Opposite*: The lower level of the elaborate balmoral suite.

Born into a seafaring family, Ron's merchant navy career began at the age of fifteen aboard training ship HMS *Conway* in North Wales. He first sailed with the Port Line, trading cargo out to Australia and New Zealand. Awarded his Second Mate's certificate in 1961, he worked on several cargo vessels. But it was a pivotal tour of duty as Fourth Officer aboard Royal Mail Line's *Andes* in the mid-sixties that, fortuitously for us, convinced the young officer that passenger ships lay undeniably in his future.

Steady promotion continued. Chief Officer Ron Warwick served aboard another cargo vessel in 1967 and obtained his Master's Ticket the following year. In 1971, he signed on with the Cunard Line, appointed

Above: Commodore Ron Warwick, bearded and beloved master of *Queen Mary 2*, shown here on board *QE2*. *Opposite*: *Queen Mary 2*'s hefty bow and bridge screen are capped by that monumental bridge.

junior officer aboard *Carmania*. Assignments aboard a flotilla of Cunarders followed until, in 1986, he assumed command of *Cunard Princess*.

The timing of his initial Cunard tour back in 1970 is important. The year previous had seen the debut of *Queen Elizabeth 2*. Sailing as master of that third *Queen* was Ron's father, Captain Bil Warwick—not William, not Bill but, decisively, Bil. A genial and beloved master, Bil Warwick founded, in effect, a remarkable shipboard dynasty. Bearded Warwick senior retired from *QE2* in 1972; eighteen years later, bearded Warwick junior became *QE2's* master. A remarkable and unique succession: in the annals of merchant shipping history, no father and son have ever commanded the same ocean liner. Ron's appointment coincided with the auspicious visit of Her Majesty Queen Elizabeth and His Royal Highness Prince Philip aboard the flagship to celebrate Cunard's sesquicentennial at Spithead in July 1990.

Crowning honors followed. In March 1998, near the end of *QE2's* world cruise, then-president Larry Pimentel and COO Pamela Conover flew to Cape Town for an onboard meeting with Captain Warwick. There, they asked him if he would delay his retirement to bring out the new ship.

"As you can imagine," Ron wrote me some years later, "it was a great honor just to be asked. The only person I told was my wife Kim. I didn't even mention it to my father before he died." That failure to share the monumental news with Bil Warwick before his sudden and unexpected death troubles his son, knowing how thrilled the old man would have been. At the same time, Captain Paul Wright was designated relief master for *Queen Mary 2*.

On March 13, 2003, with his new ship's hull already afloat in St.-Nazaire, Captain and Mrs. Warwick disembarked from *Queen Elizabeth 2* for the last time at Kobe, in the midst of her 2003 world cruise. He shared details of final chores aboard their beloved vessel: "Kim blew the whistle and I painted the funnel."

Now, let us take temporary leave of Ron Warwick and his exciting new command, relinquishing modern-day Cunard to review the company's history. As the vital work continues apace at St.-Nazaire, we must return to the early nineteenth century and document the genesis of this durable North Atlantic institution.

Sir Samuel's Novel Service

From Halifax came Joe Cunard
His father worked in the Navy Yard;
But his brother Sam made the neighbors stare
They said he would be a millionaire.

—Anonymous Halifax doggerel

Samuel Cunard's unassailable niche in mercantile history is assured forever. The shipping line he founded in 1840 revolutionized transatlantic passenger life, the first steamship service connecting Great Britain with North America.

The word "service" is significant. Deployment of four transatlantic paddle wheelers within seven months was unprecedented. These were not experimental steamships but a fleet of identical packets. From 1840 on, a Cunarder sailed westbound every fortnight delivering Royal Mail to North America.

Although the Cunards became Canadian by choice, their forebears were descendants of German Quakers who settled in Pennsylvania's Germantown in 1683. Samuel's great-great-grandfather was Thones Kunder. (The family name metamorphosed from Kunder to Conrad to Cunrad and finally to Cunard.) Thones's great-grandson Abraham established a successful shipping company. But when the colonies declared their independence, staunch loyalist Abraham Cunard's fleet and warehouses were confiscated. Ruined, he fled to Canada.

Halifax was a haven for exiles abandoning the rebellious colonies. Reduced from ship-owner to laborer, Abraham Cunard worked as a carpenter at Halifax's Royal Naval Dockyard. He married fellow loyalist Margaret Murphy, a Roman Catholic exiled from South Carolina.

Their second son, Samuel, was born on November 21st, 1787, middle sibling between Joseph and Henry. Samuel attended Halifax Grammar School and proved an astute young entrepreneur. He would buy damaged coffee and spice shipments at auction, wrap the residue into little packets and peddle them door-to-door. Later, Samuel went to Boston apprenticed to a shipbroker. Three years later he returned to Halifax, age 21, to work for newly established Abraham Cunard & Son. The firm prospered, thanks to a welcome infusion of capital realized from a prize ship.

In 1814, he and his father established a mail service between Halifax, Boston, Newfoundland, and Bermuda. That same year, Samuel married Susan Duffus who bore him two sons and seven daughters before leaving him a widower ten years later. The firm of A. Cunard & Son fielded a growing fleet, among

them the *Margaret, Nancy,* and *White Oak.* The latter was Cunard's first transatlantic vessel in 1813.

Shortly after his favorite son's marriage, Abraham Cunard relinquished control of A. Cunard & Son to Samuel, and the company reverted simply to S. Cunard. By 1827, at the age of forty, Samuel was an influential and highly respected millionaire. He was described by a fellow Haligonian as "vigorous in frame with exceptional nerve force and great powers of endurance; brisk of step, brimful of energy and always on the alert."

The burgeoning possibilities of a steamship service intrigued him. In 1833, he was one of 144 subscribers who underwrote construction of paddle steamer *Royal William.* She crossed to Britain in a respectable seventeen days, surpassing older, canvas-driven rivals. Throughout the mid-1830s, Cunard's forty-ship fleet

Above: Sir Samuel Cunard, the man who revolutionized transatlantic passenger service. *Opposite*: *Britannia* crossed in the summer of 1840, the first of dozens of Cunarders to follow.

distributed the Royal Mail that, dispatched from Falmouth on England's south coast, docked six weeks later at King's Wharf in Halifax. The laggardly performance of these superannuated, ten-gun brigs galled Samuel Cunard. Inspired by *Royal William*'s success, he wanted to supplant the Admiralty's archaic mail ships with something more up-to-date.

He was not alone. In 1838, the Lord Commissioner of the Admiralty solicited tenders for a steam service to carry the North American mails. The seven-year contract would oblige successful candidates to dispatch a mail ship every fortnight between Liverpool, Halifax, and Boston in return for an annual subsidy of £55,000.

No American shipping line responded and only two rival British companies did. Attracting neither Boston nor Halifax investors, Cunard crossed immediately for Britain. There, he raised £270,000 from a trio of Scots— David McIver, George Burns, and Robert Napier. The first two were shipping men while Napier was, fortuitously, a Glaswegian shipbuilder.

Of the thirty-three partners, Samuel Cunard was the largest investor. The selected company name said it all—The British & North American Royal Mail Steam Packet Company; passengers would call it simply

"the Cunard Line". First of the class *Britannia*, built by Robert Duncan of Greenock, was launched on February 5, 1840. Displacing 1,140 tons, she was 200 feet (61 meters) overall with a 32-foot (9.75-meter) beam. She was rigged as a three-masted barque and could accommodate 115 passengers. Two side-lever engines were installed amidships, producing 420 horsepower. Twenty-eight foot (8.5 meters) diameter paddle wheels revolved sixteen times a minute. Daily coal consumption was 40 tons, mandating bunkers accommodating 640 tons.

Sister-ship *Acadia* entered service a month after *Britannia*, on August 4, 1840. *Caledonia* first sailed September 19, and the fourth, *Columbia*, embarked her first passengers on January 5, 1841. A Cunarder steamed out of Liverpool on the fourth and nineteenth of every month but during November, December, January, and February, when they sailed only on the fourth. Of the four, *Acadia* was the most successful, holding the Blue Ribband for five years.

Above: Shown here in its glass case aboard *Queen Elizabeth 2*, the Boston Cup has been transferred to replacement flagship *Queen Mary 2*.

*Steamers properly built and manned might start
and arrive at their destination with the punctuality
of railway trains on land…We have no tunnels to drive,
no cuttings to make, no roadbeds to prepare. We need
only build our ships and start them to work.*

—Samuel Cunard

After one year, Cunard found his costs too high and obtained a subsidy increase to £81,000, on the condition that a fifth steamer be added. She was *Hibernia*, eight feet longer than her fleet-mates and accommodating 120 passengers rather than 115.

Cunard's enthusiasm was coupled with exemplary thoroughness. He signed the mail contract, built and manned his first vessel and achieved its maiden voyage within sixteen months. Although he ordained ships and crews of the first rank—"nothing but the best ships, the best officers and the best men"—a bedrock of stubborn, Haligonian practicality lay beneath. Shipbuilders were advised: "I want a plain and comfortable boat, not the least unnecessary expense for show." All five vessels' names ended with the letters "-ia," establishing a consistent naming policy for nearly a century.

Britannia sailed from Liverpool on July 4, 1840. The sixty-three passengers embarked included the founder and one of his daughters. In command of ninety crewmen was Captain Henry Woodruff, R.N. The final cargo loaded was the precious mail, delivered so late that it was 2:30 P.M. before *Britannia* sailed. Twelve days and ten hours later, she entered Halifax Harbor. Although she had carried a Halifax pilot from England, *Britannia* ran briefly aground in his harbor. Only eight hours later, *Britannia* pressed on to Boston. She arrived two days later on July 18, having completed a record crossing—two weeks and eight hours.

Britannia's late-night arrival dampened the city's reception. But three days later, Boston proclaimed "Cunard Festival Day" and 2,300 attended a banquet in Cunard's honor. Captain Woodruff was presented with a giant silver loving cup which, identified ever since as The Boston Cup, remains a cherished company relic.

Nautically, steam was unsettling. For centuries, canvas, spars, blocks, masts, and cordage had driven the world's ships. Now that pristine technology was disrupted by coal, machinery, noise, and smoke. Welsh anthracite permeated the vessel with gritty dust. Boiler room heat parched the ships' timbers, which required hosing down regularly. Paradoxically, dry rot was more pernicious in steamers than sailing vessels; according to one chief, their wooden hulls started sagging amidships after relatively few years of service.

Alien hands came aboard. These engineers, stokers, wipers, coal passers, and water tenders were atypical crewmen of sallow-complexion who toiled away from mid-ocean sun. Traditional sailors—shellbacks—resented these intruders and a Liverpool waterfront jibe disparaged "sailors who gave up the sea to go into steam."

Paddle wheels—protected by ocean-going fenders called sponsons—awkwardly increased the vessel's beam. Under way, if prevailing winds blew on the port beam, low-sided starboard paddles took a deeper bite of water, skewing the hull slightly to port. Helmsmen learned to compensate for that continuous deflection. Entering harbor, forward vantage points were obscured by raised sponsons. A catwalk bridge was added to connect the two flanking half-rounds, permitting the master to cross quickly from port to starboard: hence the origin of today's bridge.

One sobering aspect of Cunard's nascent fleet was its vulnerability. Winter crossings were so fearsome that Cunard's rivals eschewed them altogether. Sailing westbound in January 1842, *Britannia*'s starboard sponson was so trashed by gales that the naked paddles churned salt spray up onto the funnel. One lifeboat was shattered. In the summer of 1843, eastbound *Columbia* was reported two days overdue at Halifax. The worrisome wait ended only after *Acadia*, inbound from Liverpool, resolved the mystery. She had spied *Columbia* pinioned on a Seal Island reef called the Devil's Limb. Although all eighty-three passengers and crew were rescued and every precious mail sack retrieved, *Columbia* was a total loss. Six years later, *Hibernia* came to temporary grief, grounding off Cape Cod so badly that she had to return to New York for repairs.

But regardless, the service was exemplary. The line's motto was "Speed, Comfort, and Safety" and it was the third watchword that obsessed the founder. His instructions to Cunard masters were unequivocal: "Your ship is loaded, take her; speed is nothing, follow your own road, deliver her safe, bring her back safe—safety is all that is required." Outbound Cunarders crossed at latitude 43 degrees north and adhered to 42 on their return. That strict sixty-mile separation persisted through the final voyages of both *Queens*.

Thanks to Samuel's prudence, the Cunard Line gained the invaluable sobriquet "the company that never lost a life." An Atlantic legend had begun.

King of the Atlantic

As things stand now, it is scarcely possible,
in the absence of any remarkable invention,
that the speed of our Atlantic voyages
can be materially increased.

—*The Times of London,* August 27, 1852

Samuel Cunard's over-riding preoccupation was the mail, his human cargo of secondary importance. Though the word "passenger" was conspicuously absent from his contract, rules about mail were fulsomely articulated.

The Royal Navy Mail Officer was God. Assigned to every Cunarder, he could, if he deemed it necessary, override the master. No ship sailed without his approval. Prompt departures and arrivals were mandatory and severe fines were imposed for delays.

Small wonder that Samuel Cunard fretted about schedules. Hazards beyond his control included hurricanes, winter gales, summer fogs, and the probability of Boston's harbor icing over. In January 1843, it froze solid, bottling up everything in port. Bostonians cut a seven-mile channel to the sea buoy so that *Britannia* could sail, accompanied by cheering outriders on skates and sleighs. But, a lesson learned, Cunard transferred operations to New York. Though crossings were made longer, the ice-free Hudson offered incalculable advantages. Rivals to come would duplicate his pioneering move.

Cunard's shipboard accommodations were scarcely luxurious, onboard ambiance more Spartan than Lucullan. In truth, cosseting was unnecessary because throughout the 1840s Cunard's was the only game in town. Typically, the company provided no table napkins. "Going to sea," opined David MacIver, "is a hardship . . . If people want to wipe their mouths at a ship's table, they can use their pocket handkerchief." However bleak that regime, Cunard's incomparable trade-off was guaranteed arrival.

Ambitious competitors sought to capitalize on Cunard's bare-bones indifference and abrogate the front-runner's monopoly. One such was Edward Knight Collins, an American shipping mogul whose coastal packets were famously elegant. Flush with a fortune from that trade, Collins determined to surpass Cunard.

After obtaining a Congressional mail subsidy in 1850, his first transatlantic steamship, *Atlantic,* reached Liverpool in record time. By year's end, three additional Collins Line vessels—*Baltic, Arctic,* and *Pacific*—had entered service. All larger than Cunarders, they boasted the North Atlantic's first vertical cutwaters. A red racing stripe encircled their hulls and twin mermaids supported Triton figureheads. Funnel livery was, impertinently, the inverse of Cunard's—black shafts with a vibrant red band at the summit.

Averaging a brisk twelve knots, Collins vessels offered steam heating as well as interior decoration several cuts above Cunard's. Rose- and satinwood paneling, extravagant upholstery and beveled plate-glass mirrors enriched the saloon; the barbershop came with an elevating hydraulic chair. But to be fair, Collins's extravagant décor was deployed mainly for in-port show. Once Sandy Hook or Mersey lightships had been cleared, brocade and crystal were supplanted by mundane canvas and tin. But rest assured, napkins adorned every dining saloon place.

Since impatient travelers invariably patronize faster ships, Collins achieved early, gratifying success. But though his engines and luxury may have outclassed Cunard, levels of seamanship did not. On September 27, 1854, *Arctic* was rammed by the French steamer *Vesta* in fog sixty-five miles off Cape Race. The wooden American hull was fatally skewered by the Frenchman's formidable iron prow. Collins's crew reacted ineptly. Though some tried saving their ship, most made for the boats. The sole lifeboat rescued by the barque *Huron* carried fourteen passengers and thirty-four crew, an appalling ratio. The death toll of 322 souls included Collins's wife and two children.

Worse was to come: *Pacific* was posted missing with all hands two years later. With half his fleet sunk, Edward Collins lost public confidence and the Collins Line went belly up. Sir Samuel's fleet resumed transatlantic pre-eminence. (That American challenge proved curiously prescient. A century later, Cunard White Star's *Queen Mary* would be similarly humbled by a Yankee upstart when legendary *United States* captured the Blue Ribband in 1952.)

Although it was the Admiralty's considered opinion that an iron hull would sink, metal steamers proved inescapable because wooden ribs and planking could not withstand the relentless underwater thrust of the screws. The first iron Cunarder—*Andes* of 1852—was also propeller-driven. Four years after her maiden voyage, she was one of several Cunarders placed under government charter to carry regiments out to the Crimea. Indeed,

Opposite: But the smoking room's coal fire guaranteed passengers a cozy retreat during a winter North Atlantic crossing.

such was the fleet's wartime attrition that weekly mail service was, temporarily, relinquished. One bonus of that trooping charter was that Queen Victoria conferred a knighthood on the founder in 1859.

Sir Samuel embraced technological advances cautiously. For example, he and his partner Burns disagreed about adopting the propeller. Cunard felt that paddle wheels achieved faster passage. As a result, *Persia* of 1856, complete with iron hull, still sported paddles. At 390 feet (118 meters), she was more than twice *Britannia*'s size, displacing 3,300 tons instead of 1154.

The company's last paddle wheeler was *Scotia*, sailing in tandem with propeller-driven *China*. Comparison of coal consumption and speed between the two bear out Samuel Cunard's contention: *China* burned 82 tons of coal a day for a speed of 12 1/2 knots against *Scotia*'s 164 tons that produced a superior average of 14 knots. *China* also incorporated Cunard's first steerage quarters for immigrants, the thin edge of a shipboard class wedge that would grow to staggering proportions by century's end.

In 1863, a heart attack forced Cunard into London retirement, leaving his sons Edward and William in control. Two years later, within the same week that saw President Lincoln's assassination, Sir Samuel died follow-ing a severe attack of bronchitis. Seventy-eight years old, he left not only a substantial fortune of £350,000 but unquestionably the most venerated name in transatlantic history.

Immediately, a grieving board of directors convened at Liverpool headquarters, never more in need of their deceased founder's wisdom. The Cunard Line was entering an era of siege, tumult, and, ultimately, change. The Atlantic was no longer its exclusive domain; others were intent on usurping the front-runner. Formidable British rivals were steaming out of Liverpool, vessels of the Inman, Guion, Leyland, and White Star lines.

Additional competition materialized from abroad. Two-funneled *Washington* had departed Le Havre for New York in 1854, pioneer vessel of the *Compagnie Générale Transatlantique* or French Line. Further east, the Hamburg American Line entered the steamer *Borussia* of 1856 into service. That same year, the Dutch dispatched the first of ultimately six *Rotterdams* to New York. North German Lloyd's *Bremen* blazed a sea trail westbound from Bremerhaven. *Pennsylvania* sailed eastbound, the first American Line steamer. Some of these foreign upstarts initially ordered ships from British yards but they soon learned to build their own.

Cunard's directors revamped their building and out-fitting priorities. The company's bare-bones passage—

however safe—was upgraded. In one sense, it was Cunarders' increased displacement that permitted incorporation of additional public rooms and promenades, but in another, improvements were spurred by the competition.

In 1881, *Servia* was illuminated with rudimentary electric light. Refrigerated provision rooms followed three years later aboard a new pair of 8,120-ton Cunard sisters, *Etruria* and *Umbria*. These were long, racy two-stackers, their towering funnels seemingly ready to shrug off the sailing masts deployed fore and aft. Cunard dubbed the pair "The Wonder Ships": "No vessels ever gave their owners less uneasiness than these two."

Below decks, while the drawing room was separate from the dining saloon, the ladies enjoyed a music room and a smoking room accommodated gentlemen. Cabins were larger and a surrounding promenade rivaled the best of the White Star Line.

The final decade of the nineteenth century witnessed the most remarkable amplification of Cunard tonnage.

Displacing 12,950 tons, giants *Lucania* and *Campania* of 1893 were capable of 21 knots, the first vessels to shatter the North Atlantic's hitherto 20-knot ceiling.

The new class emerged as pure steamships, their secret weapon concealed beneath overhanging counters: twin propellers. If one were damaged or lost, port could still be achieved with the survivor. Canvas vanished and sailing steamers joined paddle steamers on the scrap heap of North Atlantic redundancy. With no rigging to restrict the height of deckhouses, *Campania* and *Lucania* superstructure rose heavenward, establishing the profile of the classic steamer.

Astonishingly, there was no wheelhouse for helmsmen; throughout winter crossings especially, they were exposed to the cruelest elements. Yet however Spartan the bridge, civilized comfort reigned below, including drawing rooms, libraries, and smoking rooms of increased dimension and substantial furnishing. Situated deep in the hull for stability, the dining saloon was illuminated by daylight from a vast mid-ship skylight. Connecting the two mastheads, Marconi aerials ensured miraculous mid-ocean reception of news from shore as well as communication with other vessels.

Here at the end of the nineteenth century, it is worth pausing to review shipboard's momentous changes between 1840 and 1900.

Nineteenth Century
Cunard Shipboard

The crew, on the whole, are jolly good fellows,
willing to oblige and be obliged, being always ready
to take a quarter out of you if they can.

—Advice to an American undergraduate about to embark aboard *Campania*

Return to the beginning. Share an eastbound passage aboard *Britannia*, embarking at her East Boston pier. Pack warm, serviceable clothing within your steamer trunk: nothing too fine or delicate, because you are to be confined within a noisome ethos of pervasive smells, spills, stains, and damp with only primitive washing facilities.

Your cabin is minuscule, two narrow bunks one above the other, paralleling an iron-hard horsehair sofa. Clothing must be stored in your steamer trunk parked beneath the sofa. Finery destined for London should be segregated within another trunk consigned to the hold.

A covered chamber pot is essential, for *Britannia*'s on-deck lavatories involve an invariably damp nocturnal excursion. Only one stewardess can be found. The solitary night steward's task, at 10:00 P.M., is to extinguish the candle burning within a glass-paned compartment between abutting cabins. Reveille is a barnyard chorus —a cow and goat for fresh milk, hens for eggs, and lambs for lunch.

Apart from a negligible Ladies Drawing Room, the Saloon is the sole public room, its long tables flanked by reversible benches. In rough weather, the oilcloth surface duplicates a skating pond. Raised barriers lining the tables' edge are called fiddles; they keep plates on the table but not soup in a bowl.

Inescapable *Britannia* leitmotif is a tintinnabulation of shattering china; hence, platters, plates, and mugs are the stoutest possible. The chief steward's notice reads: "Passengers unsure of their ability to complete their meal should occupy the end seat on the bench." Positioned thus, the seasick can reach the rail before divesting themselves of what Cunard characterizes euphemistically as "a tribute to Neptune."

Food is plentiful. Breakfast, at 6:00 A.M., might be steak washed down with a bottle of hock. Heralded by the jangle of a hand bell, lunch appears at 1 P.M. with an early dinner to follow at 5 P.M.

There is nowhere to roam. Gentlemen enjoy a postprandial cheroot on deck, huddled for warmth around engine room skylights. Below, passenger options include either the cabin's isolation or within that perennial shipboard beehive, the Saloon. Stewards replace mealtimes' oilcloth with green baize for companionable games of whist. Chained to the wall is a

piano at which amateur players entertain their fellow passengers to distraction. Every Sunday, when the master conducts divine services, the instrument accompanies heartfelt choruses of hymns.

Since there is nowhere to sit out on deck, foresighted passengers pack folding campstools; later, they will bring their own deck chairs and steamer rugs. A rare benefit of paddle steamers is that in fair weather, passengers can clamber atop sponsons for a unique view of their ship plowing through the waves.

Britannia can be prey to terrifying motion. The exhaustion of merely keeping erect, climbing companionways, sitting at table, or trying to sleep is challenging. Even when calm, it is noisy. Since paddle wheel shafts must project above sea level, engines are high in the vessel, cheek by jowl with cabins. Plainly heard is the crunch of the stoker's shovel, the gasping counterpoint of feed pumps, hissing steam expelled at pistons' apogee, the rumble of rotating shaft and the ceaseless "chunking" (Rudyard Kipling's apt descriptive) of paddles churning their way to Liverpool.

Having survived that *Britannia* crossing, embark for another aboard *Campania* six decades later. Now four complete decks are at your disposal, including a covered promenade beneath a row of lifeboats suspended overhead. Things are blessedly quieter. Engine noise, coal dust, and "chunking" are no more.

Cabins are higher above water and more lavishly furnished. They smell pleasantly of paint, beeswax, and flowers rather than steam, vomit, and disinfectant. There is a tip-up sink, dressing table, bureau, and wardrobe, all aglow with electric light. A brass bed replaces the bunk.

Private bathrooms are almost non-existent. Every passenger must traipse down cabin alleyways to bathe. Bath stewards reserve tub space for half-hour increments. You lather up with special salt water soap, rinsing off with a basin of fresh water. Incidentally, whether *haut monde* or hoi polloi, parading along alleyways in dressing gowns carrying towel and sponge bag is utterly *de rigeur*.

Opposite: Splendid nineteenth-century dining perquisite: *Campania* boasted a skylight that admitted daylight down through three decks.

*At night—the beauties of a night on shipboard!—down in your berth,
with the sea hissing and fizzing, gurgling and booming, within an inch of your
ear; and then the steward comes along at twelve o'clock and puts out your light,
and there you are! Jonah in the whale was not darker or more dismal.*

—Harriet Beecher Stowe, *Night on Shipboard*, 1854

But however acceptable bath-bound dishabille, the bar of sartorial shipboard has been raised for dining. Primitive haberdashery of 1840s vintage—steamer tweeds and flannels—has been replaced by satin, velvet, bombazine, and brocade. Once the bugle sounds, dressed-up passengers assemble in a dining saloon that dispenses food exclusively, serenaded by a band of steward/musicians.

Electric refrigeration guarantees a lavish selection of meats: veal, pork, ham, bacon, turkey, goose, duck, calves head, and occasional fowls and game. Additionally, there are curries, stews, and fricassees. Desserts include custards, tarts, pies, puddings and, summertime boon, ice cream, and sorbet. You still dine at long tables, face to face with fellow passengers. But you are seated now in individual swivel chairs, chair-backs carved with a Cunard lion. Fiddles are still there but less used.

Breakfast is consumed from 8:00 A.M. until 9:30 A.M., luncheon from 12:00 P.M. to 1 P.M., and dinner is on the table at 4:00 P.M. "Tea" is dispensed from 7:30 on, with late-night cocoa a Cunard staple. Having lunched or dined, passengers enjoy a choice of brightly illuminated public rooms, a smoking room for gentlemen and a drawing room for ladies and children.

Campania and *Lucania* are without question the world's fastest, 600 feet (182 meters) overall that cross in a record five days, seven hours, and twenty-three minutes. During nine consecutive summer voyages, *Lucania* averages an impressive five hundred miles each day.

The vessel boasts five decks, four indoors and one out, the topmost one called—inexplicably—the Shade Deck. A skylight between the two funnels admits light down through Shade, Promenade, and Upper Deck to the Saloon sited on Main. Daylight illuminates a splendid dining chamber 100 by 60 feet (30 x 18 meters) paneled with Spanish mahogany and beveled mirrors.

Campania and *Lucania* Promenade Decks are furnished with deck chairs and steamer rugs that passengers rent for four shillings ($1.00) the crossing. Deck stewards are in attendance, a new breed of wind-bronzed company stalwarts, hard working and sociable, their brass buttons tinged green from salt. They stage manage promenade deck affairs, setting up chairs, shrouding their occupants with steamer rugs, dispensing morning bouillon, afternoon tea, weather advisories, and seasick remedies.

In sum, *Campania* and *Lucania* offer hundreds of up-to-date cabins to suit every purse. Unrivaled for crossing time, these great Cunarders attract legions of discriminating cabin passengers as well as thousands of immigrants anxious for a new life in the New World.

But however roseate Cunard's twentieth century dawn, it had been sullied by seismic tremors from across the North Sea.

Above left: A rough ocean passage separates a smug steward from his distraught passengers. *Above, right*: The world's largest liner, *Campania,* tied up at Liverpool. Five-day crossings had arrived. *Opposite*: An *Umbria* passenger list cover.

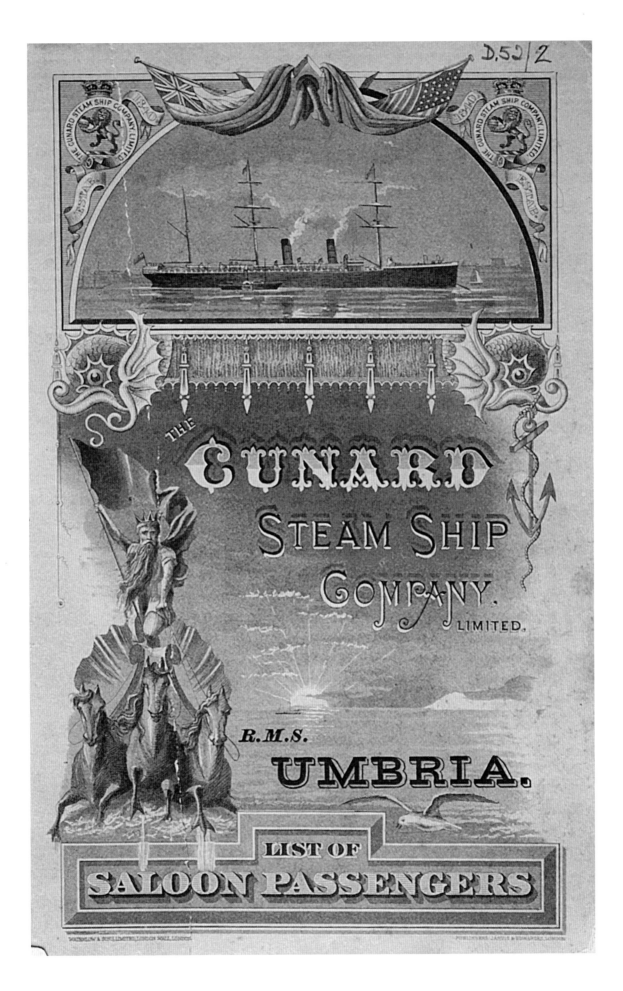

THE
CUNARD
STEAM SHIP
COMPANY.
LIMITED.

R.M.S.
UMBRIA.

LIST OF
SALOON PASSENGERS

Teutonic Challenge, Cunard Response

There was never a time in the history of Atlantic steaming
in which there was a pair of steamers so far ahead of all rivals
as the great Cunarders are now. It is the Campania and Lucania
first and no second in sight...

—The North British Daily Mail, 1894

Mark the word "response." The North Atlantic's most ambitious newbuildings were specifically wrought responses to existing record-breakers. The bleak reality was that the next dazzling newcomer would inevitably eclipse every champion's moment in the sun.

In 1897, North German Lloyd's sleek *Kaiser Wilhelm der Grosse* was that dazzling newcomer, effectively toppling Cunard's transatlantic hegemony. She combined speed with ravishing opulence. Topped with four funnels and averaging 22.35 knots, she crossed in five days, seven hours and eight minutes, co-opting both Blue Ribband and the cream of North Atlantic traffic. *Lucania* and *Campania* were suddenly also-rans, surpassed by crack vessels of not one but two German rivals; Hamburg America Line's *Deutschland* proved even faster than *Kaiser Wilhelm der Grosse*.

A combination of jingoism, hubris, and a desire for revenge mandated John Bull's response. A parliamentary subsidy of £2,600,000 allowed Cunard to construct two superliners, *Lusitania* and *Mauretania*. Each was capable of 24.5 knots, specifically exceeding *Deutschland*'s top of 23.5 knots.

New prime movers were contemplated. Once Sir Charles Parsons had demonstrated the efficacy of his phenomenal *Turbinia* in 1897, Cunard determined to employ turbines in both superliners. A preliminary test was devised aboard *Caronia* and *Carmania* of 1905, subsequently nicknamed "The Pretty Sisters." Whereas twin-screwed *Caronia* was powered by reciprocating engines, *Carmania*'s three propellers were shafted to turbines. After a year's deployment, *Carmania* averaged one knot faster. For *Lusitania* and *Mauretania*, turbines were the obvious answer. Construction contracts were signed, with *Lusitania* to be built at John Brown's Yard on the Clyde and *Mauretania* at Swan, Hunter, & Whigham Richardson at Wallsend-on-Tyne.

Take note of a significant newbuilding dimension, the height of a vessel's visible flank from boot-topping to boat deck. It betrayed not only deck proliferation but public room pretension as well. The taller-ship vogue achieved glorious fruition aboard *Lusitania* and *Mauretania* of 1907. Here were public rooms twelve feet high, ceilings ennobled by skylights with richly gadrooned plaster surrounds. Company décor had metamorphosed into a serene, country house pastiche.

Glaswegian architect James Millar created Cunard's first double-decked dining saloon aboard *Lusitania*. Whereas the main lounge was mahogany-paneled Georgian, the Adam writing room/library was dominated by an enormous breakfront after Chippendale. Only his smoking room forsook a light palette, clad instead with dark Italian walnut.

This last was similar to Englishman Harold Peto's *Mauretania* treatment. He ordained an oak, Francois Premier dining room, a smoking room paneled with intricately carved mahogany, and a main lounge infused with the Gallic exhilaration of Louis XVI.

In *The Song of the Machines*, Rudyard Kipling characterized *Mauretania* as a "monstrous nine-decked city." Of those nine, six were for passengers, in descending order. First class public rooms were sixty feet (eighteen meters) above the sea. Small wonder that both superliners boasted twin elevators, their grills wrought of weight-saving aluminum.

Lusitania was undeniably the prototype—first launched, first fitted out, and first to achieve New York landfall in September 1907. She was christened by Mary, Lady Inverclyde, widow of Cunard's late chairman. The launch was unprecedented; *Lusitania*'s 16,000-ton empty hull displaced more than *Kaiser Wilhlem der Grosse* fitted out. Once the champagne shattered, *Lusitania* stirred, her purposely glacial momentum down to the Clyde never exceeding seven feet per second. Two full minutes elapsed before her 790 feet were safely afloat.

Her rearward surge was arrested by bundled crescents of 1861 *Great Eastern*'s anchor cable. How fitting that remnants of Brunel's giant should usher *Lusitania* into life; she was the first liner exceeding *Great Eastern*'s displacement.

Rather than sister ships, *Lusitania* and *Mauretania* were consorts, dissimilar products of two competing yards. *Lusitania*'s profile seemed racier, boasting apparently greater funnel height because her "ashcan" ventilators were so low.

Opposite: A decorative but ominous poster from North German Lloyd introduces a devastating new competition for Cunard. *Overleaf:* Arriving in New York for the first time, *Lusitania* attracted throngs of excited New Yorkers to Cunard's pier.

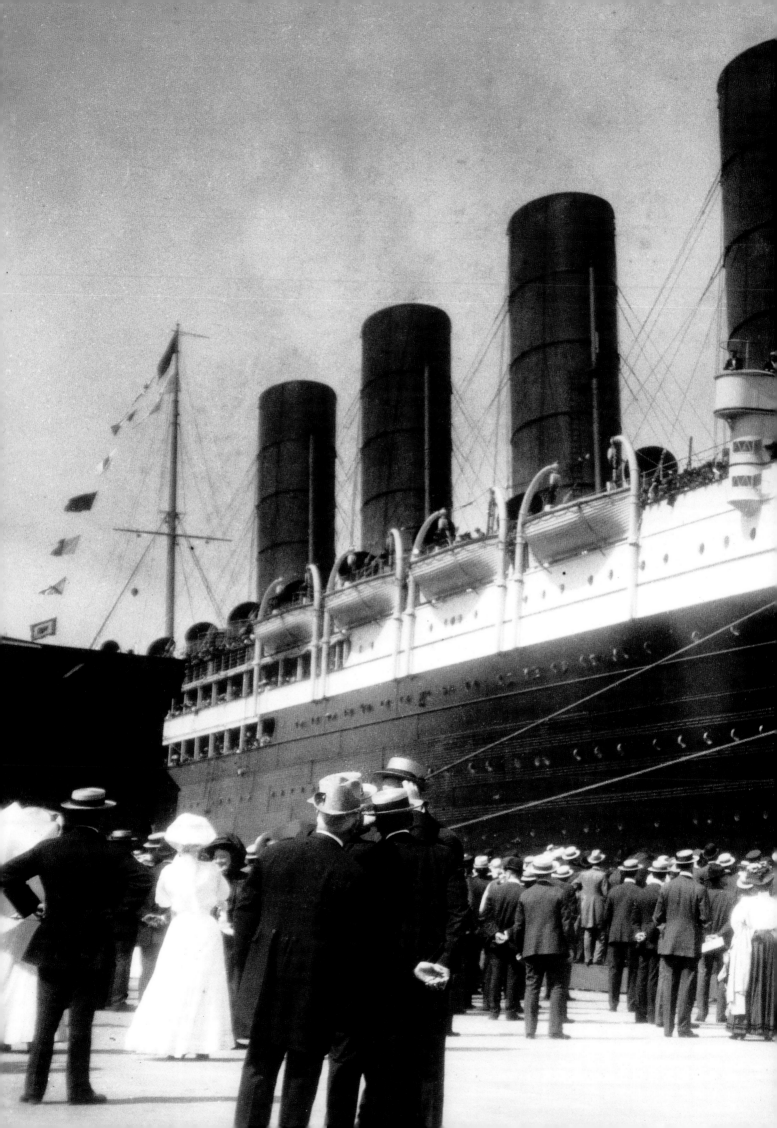

Lusitania would be sunk by a torpedo off Ireland's southern tip on May 7, 1915, a tragedy that has indelibly stigmatized her. To my mind, she deserves remembrance less for her demise than her landmark design. Rather than scatter classes throughout the hull, strict vertical segregation was implemented instead: First class amidships, second aft and third forward.

First Class was surrounded by two promenade decks. Only via the uppermost deck could passengers circumnavigate the hull. Second class passengers were accommodated in the after 150 feet of hull—stacked within their own vertical honeycomb—and third class occupied the bow. Their cabins were packed densely forward on the main and lower decks; no third class passenger ever ascended above shelter deck. *Lusitania*'s pioneering GA encompassed a more complex spread of interlocking classes than Cunard had ever dealt with before.

In New York, though the Corps of Engineers strove to finish brand-new Ambrose Channel for the superliners, it would resist completion until August 1909. Incomplete too for *Lusitania*'s maiden arrival was Cunard's

longer Pier 54 when, on September 13, 1907, she steamed triumphantly into New York. Despite fog off Cape Race, she averaged just under twenty-four knots. Two years later, *Mauretania* would average 26.06 knots, crossing in four days, ten hours and fifty-one minutes. The superiority of Parsons turbines proven, *Mauretania* would retain the Blue Ribband until 1929.

Neither of Cunard's dazzling consorts was really luxurious. Built for speed rather than comfort, they offered a hard ride. Gymnasium, swimming bath, and extra-tariff restaurant were not included. Construction of a third compatible superliner was unavoidable. Sailing first in 1914, *Aquitania*, at 45,000 tons, boasted half again her predecessors' displacements. She was

Above: Although Cunard's superliners were rarely together, here are both *Lusitania* and *Mauretania* berthed in the Liverpool docks. *Opposite:* Architect Harold Peto's *Mauretania* smoking room. Each evening, atop the octagonal table in the center, numbers for the mileage pool were auctioned off by a passenger chairman.

certainly no *Lusitania* clone. *Aquitania*'s larger, boxier hull accommodated 3200 passengers and substantially more cargo. Her ninety-seven-foot (thirty-meter) beam was broader than *Lusitania*'s and her superstructure denser, the funnel quartet surrounded by clustered ventilators.

Interiors were devised by Arthur Joseph Davis, a Paris-trained, Beaux-Arts architect. He created a paradigm of serene Edwardian *luxe*, including Cunard's first swimming bath and gymnasium. His Louis XVI restaurant for the first class was furnished with proper tables and chairs, the infamous swivels relegated to third. Blue carpeting replaced standard linoleum tiling. Curiously, unlike *Lusitania*'s and *Mauretania*'s double-decked dining rooms, *Aquitania* passengers dined on one level only.

Portions of both promenades were enriched by innovative garden lounges, unique enclosures suitable for tea, reading, dozing, or mid-ocean chatter. Bouillon or tea was enjoyed at wicker tables and chairs next to ivy-covered, faux stone walls. With a newcomer's refreshing effrontery, Davis had gentrified *Aquitania*'s promenades.

The main lounge they insulated was replete with Robert Adam resonances. Aft on the same deck was the Caroleon Smoking Room, the only paneled public room on board. Heroic maritime canvasses punctuated the walls. Standing lanterns were festooned with Venetian garnish and topped by dolphins to create an impressive nautical space. Although cords of *Mauretania*'s mahogany paneling were preserved, *Aquitania*'s glorious smoking room went intact to the breakers in 1950.

Perhaps Davis's most novel *Aquitania* accomplishment remains his long gallery connecting main lounge with smoking room. By placing it off center, naval architect Leonard Peskett and Davis circumvented funnel casings, transforming humdrum passage into extended parlor. That long gallery was furnished with wing chairs, side tables, and occasional card tables, creating inviting, palm-filled oases.

Aquitania's May 1914 maiden voyage averaged a respectable 23.1 knots, sufficiently compatible with her predecessors. Steaming into heavy seas, she plunged just like *Mauretania* but with restrained dignity rather than savage glee.

She straddled a critical Cunard divide. Whereas *Lusitania* and *Mauretania* were essentially ocean greyhounds like *Lucania* and *Campania*, *Aquitania* inaugurated a stupendous new scale, not only tall but also very big. Here was a floating preview of monumental displacements to come.

Above: The *Aquitania*'s Louis XVI restaurant—no longer dining saloon—was the North Atlantic's handsomest. *Opposite*: Revealing her graceful counter stern, *Aquitania* rests in Liverpool's Gladstone drydock.

Three Predecessor *Queens*

I watched the woodwork being made...fashioned by careful, exacting men whose hand cult extends back in many cases thirty or forty years at those same benches.

—E. P. Leigh-Bennet, A City Goes to Sea

Alas, Cunard's three superliners enjoyed only the briefest deployment before the guns of August 1914 aborted peacetime service. Postwar, vanished *Lusitania* was replaced by *Berengaria*, formerly HAPAG's *Imperator* awarded to Cunard as a prize of war.

In 1920, Congress curtailed unrestricted immigration, a sobering cold shower for shipping lines. Huge vessels constructed specifically for immigrant millions were suddenly redundant. Thanks to canny marketing, huge transatlantic liners were transformed to attract American tourists in upgraded third class. Because of this reverse migration, postwar traffic became overwhelmingly American rather than European.

Cunard was not alone in soliciting this lifesaving business. But as the twenties waned, competition from newer rivals did not. Cunard's primary trio was creaking Edwardian tonnage, grown long in the funnel. For postwar passengers, *Mauretania*, *Aquitania*, and *Berengaria* seemed stuffily anachronistic; moreover, the lack of private bathrooms was damaging. Up-to-date new-buildings were essential.

In January 1926, an historic meeting was convened at Cunard's Liverpool headquarters: on the agenda, a two-ship weekly mail service to North America. Twin express liners, 1,000 feet (305 meters) long, were posited to fulfill the following scenario: One sails from Southampton on Wednesday noon, calling at Cherbourg before racing westbound. After 112 hours (4 and 2/3 days) at sea, she ties up in Manhattan early Monday.

After a 50 hour turnaround, she sails at 11:00 A.M. Wednesday, a week after her Southampton departure. Proceeding eastbound for 112 hours, she arrives at Cherbourg Monday morning. A Channel crossing sees her tied up in Southampton by 3:30 P.M., primed for yet another Wednesday departure.

Implicit within that projection was a second ship sailing an identical itinerary. Thus, every Wednesday, two giant Cunarders would sail, one from Southampton, the other from New York. They would serve as immutable transatlantic pendulums, thundering eastbound and westbound year-round. A service speed of 27.61 knots would fluctuate to a maximum of 28.94 knots, depending on seasonal conditions.

The decision was taken to build the first of these revolutionary Cunarders at John Brown's yard. Hull

number 534's keel was laid with a 1932 launch anticipated. But a global depression intervened and plummeting passenger revenues crippled Cunard's cash flow. All work was halted for over two years until a parliamentary subsidy guaranteed completion. Acceptance of government assistance obliged Cunard to merge with rival White Star.

Her Majesty christened the ship with her name and the largest Cunarder to date sailed in June 1936. Although *Queen Mary*'s interiors were not necessarily daring, they were comfortable and chic. There was a capacious main lounge, rows of sleek shops, a splendid smoking room, a tiled indoor pool, and, overlooking the stern, Cunard's first extra-tariff restaurant, the Veranda Grill. An identical fixture was planned aboard *Queen Elizabeth*, scheduled to join the *Mary* in service in 1940.

Above: A second Queen Elizabeth but a third *Queen:* the last ocean liner to be launched from John Brown's historic yard was christened by Her Majesty in 1967. *Opposite:* In December 1948, the two *Queens, Mary* to the left and *Elizabeth* to the right, bracket Manhattan's Pier 90. A Southampton seamen's strike precipitated a rare joint appearance. *Overleaf:* Making her maiden entry into the port of New York, brand-new *Queen Mary* steams triumphantly up the North River toward Manhattan's specially lengthened super piers.

they crossed and recrossed year-round, the most patronized and profitable liners ever launched. Everyone who was anyone crossed on the *Mary* and the *Elizabeth*—statesmen, royalty, film stars, literati—as well as millions of ordinary passengers. Passage was inexpensive, fast, and, in the first class, fashionable. Cunard's contemporary slogan said it all: "Getting there is half the fun." To my mind, it was all the fun.

Unlike prior Cunard pairs such as *Lusitania* and *Mauretania*, the two *Queens* were distinctively different; their keels laid seven years apart. *Mary* was more traditional, her funnel trio supported by guy wires. A vertical stem and forward well deck dated her as well. The *Elizabeth* was more contemporary, with only two freestanding funnels and a rakish clipper bow. Her GA was similar but not identical, the décor adhering to a late-thirties ambiance.

In 1956 came a sinister milestone: More transatlantic passengers flew than sailed. Once crossing time could be measured in hours rather than days, passage by sea was doomed. The company withdrew both *Queens*. The *Mary* departed New York forever in September 1967, bound for California's Long Beach. She has been moored there ever since, a tenancy now surpassing her years of service.

Queen Elizabeth fared worse. Withdrawn a year later, she endured an ignominious stay in Florida's Port Everglades before being rechristened *Seawise University* and sailing to Hong Kong for refitting. But she was sabotaged by fire and Cunard White Star's former flagship burned through the night before rolling onto her starboard beam-ends, a total loss.

A new and very different successor first sailed in 1969. Suiting reality, *Queen Elizabeth 2* was a hybrid—part liner, part cruise ship, and to some, initially disappointing. Conditioned to the multi-funneled majesty of *Mary* and *Elizabeth*, this ultramodern, understated *Queen* seemed somehow shy of the mark.

War intervened. Gray-painted *Queen Elizabeth* dashed empty to New York, and shortly thereafter, both she and her consort were dragooned as troopships until 1946. In October of that year, *Elizabeth* was dispatched on her proper maiden voyage to New York. Reconverted *Mary* followed shortly thereafter and Cunard's two-ship service, conceived in 1929, was finally realized.

Throughout the balance of the forties, all of the fifties, and most of the sixties, the legendary *Queens* remained a North Atlantic institution. Like clockwork,

Above: VIPs—Very Important Passengers—disembarking from one of the *Queens* in New York include Sir Winston Churchill, Dorothy Lamour, and Cary Grant. *Opposite*: *Queen Mary*'s rivet-studded flank seen from a New York tug. Her distinctive bridge wing shelters were not duplicated aboard the *Elizabeth*.

The vessel's image, suggested naval architect James Gardner in automotive parlance, was "sleek Bentley rather than foursquare Daimler." Her profile incorporated a single, pencil-slim black pipe above a white plinth. Cunard's traditional funnel color, visible only from bridge or helicopter, had been daubed discreetly inside the surrounding aerodynamic scoop, which lofted stack gas away from passenger decks.

Although the funnel plinth was belatedly repainted with the company livery, installation of a more imposing fixture awaited Bremerhaven's 1987 refit, when a massive heart transplant converted the engines from steam turbine to diesel-electric. Nine diesel uptakes required a more substantial housing that markedly improved the vessel's summit.

Corporate buzz about the new ship betrayed a determination to distance exhilarating present from what was perceived as archaic past. Cunard was determined to shuck its patrician image. "Ships," pronounced their brutally candid marketing mantra, "have been boring long enough."

In the mother country, "swinging London" was in vogue and vanguard designer David Hicks was repainting Regency drawing rooms with his bold palette. Dennis Lennon's *Queen Elizabeth 2* interiors—walls, staircases, banisters, and upholstery—glowed with the same startling colors. Man-made materials predominated 'tween decks, relentlessly mod and remote from *Queen Mary*'s paneled, vaulted majesty. Coffee shop and disco were in, smoking room and garden lounge out. Restaurants were high in the ship. Stewards wore turtlenecks, their vessel's name abbreviated to *QE2*, a breezy logo typifying the company's informal, new guise.

No chapter documenting the three *Queens* should end without evaluating Cunard's imperial versus democratic image. Happily, since her maiden voyage, much of the grandeur that *QE2*'s designers had been instructed to eschew has reappeared. The turtlenecks are gone, restaurant managers are back in white tie and tails, royal portraits and a heritage trail enliven the staircases. Cunard's glorious history is triumphantly on view.

Equating tradition with boredom was a grievous error. In fact, Americans—the majority of *QE2*'s clientele —embark in search of the same imperial vibes that also attract them to the Royal Tattoo, Buckingham Palace, Windsor Castle, the changing of the guard—in sum, the panoply of Britain's royal mystique.

Stephen Payne has wisely observed, "Cunard without a Queen is not really Cunard." By extension, a *Queen* without elegance, grandeur, and tradition is equally unthinkable. After all, the rampant lion adorning Cunard's house flag is crowned, conveying a potent regal message. Appropriately, the company's fourth *Queen* acknowledges Cunard's imperial stance.

Above: In October 1946, *Queen Elizabeth* departs Southampton on her proper maiden voyage. *Opposite*: *QE2* with Empire State Building in foreground.

Twentieth Century Cunard Shipboard

*There is the rumble of trucks and the clump of trunks, the strident chatter
of a crane and the first salt smell of the sea. You hurry through, even though there's time.
The past, the continent, is behind you; the future is that glowing mouth in the side
of the ship; this dim turbulent gangway is too confusedly the present.*

—F. Scott Fitzgerald, *The Rough Crossing*

From 1900 until 2000, life aboard Cunard vessels accommodated itself, predictably, to advancing technology, market conditions, and passenger expectations.

That a company renowned for crossing should cruise so effortlessly was scarcely surprising. Traditionally, the Mediterranean had been the Cunard's most scenic arena; in 1912, when *Carpathia* diverted to stricken *Titanic*, she was en route to the Holy Land. But it was brand-new *Laconia* and *Samaria* that inaugurated the company's most ambitious voyages in 1922. Both departed New York that fall to circumnavigate the globe.

Once into the tropics, passengers embraced innovative warm-weather rituals: buffet luncheons on deck, canvas pools, awnings everywhere, shaded deck chairs, exotic ports, dancing under the stars, breeze-catching scuttles projecting from portholes, crews in perpetual whites and tendering to shore. A decade later, *Laconia*'s sister ship *Franconia* became the company's preeminent world cruiser.

The same depression that delayed *Queen Mary* diverted the three Edwardian stalwarts she would replace from under-booked winter crossings to popular cruises. Flocks of new passengers embarked for democratic, one-class jaunts to the West Indies, Bermuda, and the Mediterranean. *Mauretania* adopted a white hull and *Aquitania* sailed to Rio in 1938.

But the company's cruising apotheosis was achieved in the late forties with 34,000-ton, green-painted *Caronia,* which cornered the upscale market. Significantly, segments of her world cruise were not offered. This restriction encouraged such *snobbisme* and allegiance that *Caronia*'s successive world cruise passenger lists remained almost identical.

Between global peregrinations, "The Green Goddess" visited both Mediterranean and Baltic. But without fail, she disembarked her largely American clientele in Southampton on Wednesday mornings because their *Caronia* ticket included express westbound passage aboard a waiting *Queen*.

That ingenious interface of cruising *Caronia* with crossing *Queen* returns us neatly to the North Atlantic. Sail eastbound with me from Manhattan's Pier 90 for a *Queen Mary* crossing in June 1956. Across a bristly doormat, through glowing alleyways, stewards conduct you to a cabin with lavish closets and drawers, and a spacious bathroom.

Outnumbering the eighteen hundred passengers, thousands of chattering visitors overwhelm the vessel, women hatted and gloved, gentlemen seersuckered against summer's humidity. There is no air conditioning, only oscillating fans and ball-and-socket punka louvers circulating on-deck air. On the vessel's (shaded) port side, open portholes help. Fighting their way through the crush, stewards deliver champagne, ice, parcels, flowers, fruit baskets, and, always, telegrams. Their colleagues struggle with wardrobe trunks perched atop trolleys, two of which *Queen Mary*'s alleyways can accommodate *en passant*.

Brass-buttoned bellboys crying "All ashore that's going ashore!" precipitate two decisive events—visitor departure and passenger lunch. On offer are fresh Maine lobsters, reflecting westbound's first-day perquisite of England's Dover soul.

Queen Mary's alleyways are tiled with polychromatic Korkoid linoleum, and the receding squeak of sneakered children racing past is as distinctive as the lounge's chattering walls. Both *Queens* are paneled with the *boiserie* of empire. Every afternoon at four, a string orchestra plays for tea, with a musical quiz to follow.

Black ties enrich every evening save first and last. There is no cruise director, no cabaret, no production show, and limited audio equipment. Diversions include bingo, horse racing, movies, or masquerade. There is also much dancing, drinking, and, always, good talk, civilized passenger-camaraderie endemic. Friendships flower swiftly. Perhaps the best locales for passenger encounters are the enclosed promenade decks. Morning walkers tramp repeatedly past deck-chaired shipmates, to whom stewards dispense bouillon at eleven.

Newfound companions or shipmates from previous crossings share noontime drinks in the smoking room, paid for in cash, dollars or pounds; credit cards and cash-free shipboard are decades away. Lunch is served only down in C-Deck's restaurant; *Queen Mary* has no lido, indeed, no alternative catering save for the Veranda Grill or a cabin tray.

Opposite: Within a wide variety of Cunard dining rooms between the wars, passengers enjoyed superb cuisine, deft service, and stimulating conversation.

Afternoon activities vary. Though the sedentary succumb to deck-chaired siestas, the athletically inclined haunt the gymnasium. The squash court is heavily booked. The inevitable finale is a Turkish bath and massage followed by a restorative plunge into D-Deck's pool.

Long before they turn down beds and draw curtains, stewards have laid out dinner jackets. Stewardesses assist distaff passengers with zippers or buttons, summoned by a green cabin button; their male colleagues respond to red.

Paradoxically, there is nothing to do yet never enough time to do everything; five sea days pass in a contented blur. Quizzes, bridge, backgammon, shops, and library beckon. Evenings are dense with engagements as passengers accept invitations to officers' quarters for drinks. In the smoking room, main lounge, and garden lounge, stewards sustain a frantic pace during the cocktail hour.

France's approach is heralded by crew distraction, reemerging suitcases, and distribution of baggage labels, boat-train tickets, and custom forms. Addresses and itineraries are scribbled in passenger list margins. Shipboard chums will reunite throughout the UK or continent, friendships forged at sea aboard a *Queen*.

Outdoors, a northern chill replaces New York humidity. Three-toed kittiwakes circle the stern where refuse is routinely jettisoned these ecologically insensitive days. Suddenly, *Queen Mary* is alongside at Cherbourg and the passenger body fragments. That afternoon, the London-bound residue troops ashore at Southampton, with a farewell glimpse of *Mary*'s funnel trio spied above the ocean terminal. That crossing completed, another begins two days later.

A 1983 North Cape cruise aboard *Queen Elizabeth 2* rounds out last century's overview. The ocean terminal is still there, its days numbered. We embark through *QE2*'s midship lobby, encircled by a lime-green, leather sofa. Alleyways to cabins are carpeted now, Korkoid a casualty of 1960s spike heels.

Cabins are still capacious and paneled, though salt water bathing is no more; the only in-cabin sea water

---

Above left: Treasure Jones, original *Queen Mary*'s last master. After he brought her into Long Beach, he would signal FINISHED WITH ENGINES, forever. *Above right:* First-class passengers tramp around the echoing Promenade Deck, past deck-chaired shipmates. *Opposite:* This poster's subliminal message is that *Queen Mary* was not the exclusive domain of film stars and millionaires; humbler passengers were also sought.

Cunard White Star

flushes toilets. Promenades are gone too, their width absorbed into a beamier Queens Room. In addition to first class's Columbia and tourist's Tables of the World, two additional grills—Princess and Queens—are extant; no longer extra-tariff, both accommodate occupants of QE2's most expensive cabins.

Whatever the restaurant, Cunard's traditional dining expertise continues, an amalgam of deft stewards, flickering spirit lamps, and splendid menus. Every Columbia table boasts a glowing Plexiglas column illuminated from below through the cloth. My wife, Mary, and I share a window table, seated in well-balanced aluminum chairs. Throughout my first QE2 crossing in 1970, those same Columbia windows had been opaque with fog. Now, the view is idyllic. QE2-size vessels must parallel rather than skirt Norway's incomparable coastline but distant mountains enchant nonetheless.

So do the ports. At oil-rich Stavanger, the ship berths alongside the old town's sun struck roofs ascending the hills; summer heat propels passengers into both stern pools. Entry into majestic Geiranger fjord is captivating, a breathtaking panorama of limpid fjord and cliff-sides laved by the gauzy caress of the Seven Sisters waterfalls.

Across the Arctic Circle, perpetual daylight creates a surreal shipboard mood. Anchored off Honnigsvag, North Cape's port, Mary and I, in evening dress and dinner jacket respectively, loll in deck chairs at midnight, coffee tray in lap, bewitched by daylight's winsome nocturnal intrusion.

Norway's coast was the earliest cruise ships' prime destination and that midsummer Nordic magic still compels. Transatlantic urgency has been supplanted by cruising languor. It is the same blessed duality—purposeful crossing and dawdling cruise—that our fourth Queen also embodies to perfection.

With this distant hors d'oeuvre consumed, let us hasten to St.-Nazaire for *plat principale*.

Above: Viewed from atop Honolulu's Aloha Tower, second *Caronia*'s on-deck pool (*far left*) buttressed her cruising commitment. *Opposite:* Seen from astern in New York, *Queen Elizabeth 2* is topped by her post-1987 Bremerhaven funnel.

Hull G32

Today marks the beginning of the actual construction phase of our new liner, Queen Mary 2... *This is a significant milestone in the process of creating this vessel, and really starts the "clock ticking" for us all as we begin, in earnest, the countdown to delivery.*

—President Conover, cutting the first steel at St.-Nazaire on January 16, 2002,

The late William Francis Gibbs was America's foremost naval architect, perhaps best remembered for his immortal *United States* of 1952. His perennial toast amongst shipping colleagues was, "To the big ship and everything you've always wanted, doubled!" It has never been clear to which "big ship" he first referred, whether *Leviathan, America,* or *United States,* but his words served as tacit acknowledgment of the preoccupation shared by everyone involved with a newbuilding. Were Gibbs alive and toasting today, I am sure this new Cunarder would indubitably qualify as his ultimate big ship.

Queen Mary 2 began life at St.-Nazaire at the dawn of the twenty-first century. In embryo, she was dubbed by the shipyard G32, an almost unrecognizable assemblage of rectangular shapes. As she grew, that biggest big ship remained the focus of everyone concerned in Miami, London, and St.-Nazaire. All were transfixed by the monumental hull that grew into their lives as compellingly as it grew in the dry dock.

In charge was Project Manager Gerry Ellis. His career started at sea with P&O in 1978 and he joined Cunard in 1990, assigned to a rota of company vessels. He obtained his master's certificate two years later. In 1996, Chief Officer Ellis was appointed Marine Operations Manager. Shortly thereafter, he was promoted to Manager, then Director of Newbuilds, responsible, as he puts it, "for all aspects of both new ships—design, delivery, and budget." As *QM2* Project Manager, he utilized not only his extensive maritime knowledge but also reserves of patience and diplomacy. *Reductio ad absurdam,* Gerry was "our man in St.-Nazaire."

He served as shipyard liaison for fellow Cunard officers Captain Ron Warwick and Chief Engineer Simon Gillan. Additionally, he was head of a four-man inspection team made up of Cunard personnel, and also a Carnival inspection team from the company's London office. Their overriding concern: to insure that *Queen Mary 2* conformed to expectation in every respect.

Construction began with flat, steel plates spread outdoors in gently rusting rows. They are sorted by a lone Frenchman operating an electromagnetic transporter. The noise of his work is familiar—an abrupt clatter as a dozen electrified, chain-supported heads clang down onto a selected plate. Electrically glued on demand to its carrier, it is lifted and transported into a steel-cutting shed or *atelier* for incorporation into sections or, in French, *blocs.* G32 required ninety-eight *blocs* in all.

Much of the steel ordered by Chantiers de l'Atlantique was, predictably, out of the ordinary. Indeed, everything about *Queen Mary 2* tends to the exceptional. By way of elaboration, consider four steel samples adorning my study mantelpiece. The thinnest piece, at six millimeters (less than a one-quarter of an inch) makes up a souvenir profile of *Voyager of the Seas,* cut at Kvaener-MASA in October 1997. A second, cut in the shape of Royal Caribbean's crown-and-anchor, is from *Legend of the Seas,* ten millimeters (three-eighths of an inch plus). Next is a souvenir paperweight of *Queen Mary 2* steel, thicker at fifteen millimeters (a fraction under five-eighths of an inch). The fourth dates from 1958, an imposing fragment of *France*'s hull, also built at Chantiers de l'Atlantique; it is twenty-five millimeters thick (just shy of one inch), the diameter of an American twenty-five-cent piece. Second *Queen Mary*'s bow plates are, at twenty-eight millimeters, even thicker; and beneath the plating, the density and dimensions of the underlying frames are proportionately greater. Indeed, small wonder that, because of the remarkable strength of her hull, *Queen Mary 2* is described informally throughout Chantiers de l'Atlantique as "Stephen's pocket battleship."

Steel that had to be curved was passed between the rollers of hydraulic plate-bending machines, gradually wrought into specifically ordained shape. Flat sheets for decks or bulkheads were stitched together by machine welding into large panels reinforced by channel steel. However, machine welding was impossible within tightly cornered recesses. Individual welders did the job, one stitch at a time. Throughout every *atelier,* welders crouched within half-completed sections, their presence betrayed only by the brilliance of electric arcs. Hooded, gloved, and aproned against the crackling, fiery hazard of their craft, they joined plate, frame, bracket, and column into three-dimensional reality.

Opposite: Twin steel panels full of complex, compound curves betray their destination in the finished hull as both sides of the bow.

Once completed, each section was jacked up so that a yard transporter could drive beneath it. These are a yard transporter could drive beneath it. These are motorized flatbeds supported by multiple, heavy-duty tires. With the completed section on board, the *atelier's* sliding doors opened and the transporter carried it outdoors to be parked against the day of attachment.

Assembling newbuilds with prefabricated sections was a system perfected as a mass production expediency during World War II. A section is nothing more than a mammoth chunk of ship, much like an overscale Lego piece made of steel rather than plastic and sometimes weighing over 200 tons (182 metric tons).

Whether part of the double bottom, the soaring prow or a length of cabins, few sections were completed empty. All interior hardware within—bulkhead, deck, pump, tank, pipe, column—was pre-installed, placement that would prove difficult after it had been added to the hull. Uniting adjacent sections was not merely a question of marrying exterior margins but every interior sinew as well.

President Conover ceremonially cut G32's first steel on a chilly January day of 2002. She confessed that worrying about the ship meeting its promised delivery date gave her occasional sleepless nights. "It has been pointed out to me that the one surefire way to guarantee that a ship is completed on time is to make sure that the shipyard chairman is booked—*together with his wife*—on the maiden voyage." To laughter and cheers, Conover presented Chairman Patrick Boissier with two maiden voyage tickets.

Half a year later, with preliminary sections completed, it was time for keel laying, the start of actual construction. Flanking the dry dock is a large expanse called

l'aire de prémontage—the assembly area—a parking lot for completed sections. These were the lowest hull *blocs*, each one very similar to the next; only the curve of a bilge conveyed a verifiable ship shape.

Stern sections were assembled upside down. Before they could be attached, they were inverted in midair by two cranes juggling in delicate tandem, similar to children's hands exchanging and manipulating string cages while playing cat's cradle. Those juggling cranes are gantries, the yard's heaviest lifters. Straddling both dry dock and assembly area, they are enormous (inverted) U-shaped cranes that can ride the length of the dock, encompassing *l'aire de prémontage* and dry dock within their 800-ton lifting span. The horizontal top of each inverted U is the crossbeam. Completed sections can be raised upward, carried over the dock via the crossbeam and delivered the length of the hull by the gantry's rolling base.

Laying a keel in the old days was simpler; a single length of steel would be lowered atop sloping keel blocks. That was the primary hull element to which all other parts would be attached. Today, a prefabricated keel section is positioned atop keel blocks in the dry dock. On July 4, 2002—*Britannia's* sailing day from Liverpool 162 years earlier—Pam Conover spoke before a gathering of press, shipyard, and company personnel.

"To start this process, I have here a walkie-talkie and with it, that gentleman up there"—she gestured to the gantry operator far above—"can be asked to lay the section in place. But I'm not going to do that. Instead, I think it appropriate that the first master of *QM2* should today issue his first order, to lay the section of keel." Ron Warwick stepped forward and spoke authoritatively into the mouthpiece: "Crane driver, this is Captain Warwick speaking. Please commence the building of my ship!"

Moments later, combined *blocs* 502 and 503 and panel 102, weighing 650 metric tons, were lowered noiselessly into place. Concealed beneath the keel were two coins, a commemorative Golden Jubilee crown and a silver franc piece, appropriate Anglo/French talismens.

Two down, ninety-six to go. The keel section was positioned at the bottom of an enormous dry dock called Forme B, a cubic concrete ditch nearly a kilometer long. At its landward end is a ramped entryway

Opposite: Complementary curved bow hull panels, port and starboard, under construction. Fashioning precisely the right complex of curves is newbuilding skill at its most demanding. *Above left:* Pamela Conover initiates the first steel cutting at St.-Nazaire. She was nearly dunked in the process. *Above right:* Front row seats for a momentous keel-laying: (*from left to right*) Captain Warwick, Pam Conover, Patrick and Isabelle Boissier, Micky and Lynn Arison. *Overleaf:* G32's lowest, terminal stern section is about to be joined to the hull.

Queen Mary 2

permitting descent to the puddled, rust-stained concrete floor. At the other end, pumps can flood or drain the dock. It is flooded either to move a partially built hull further down dock or to free it from Forme B forever. For this second alternative, an opening caisson gives access to the Loire.

Halfway along Forme B's length is a giant step down. The upper portion, furthest from the exit, is for nascent hulls. Once sufficient sections of that hull have been conjoined for buoyancy, the dock is flooded, and the embryonic vessel winched down over duplicate keel blocks on the lower level.

Today's newbuildings no longer slide down banisters into the sea. That hurtling drama, historically a moment of angst, celebration, and christening, has been supplanted by a surreptitious lift off the keel blocks. G32's float-off occurred one weekend night, December 1, 2002, nearly five months after the keel laying. The hull had not yet achieved its ultimate bullet configuration but seemed more like an ungainly barge.

In preparation for that first move, G32-as-barge was laden with some vital cargo. Four diesels and their alternators were installed, as were six Carrier chillers, shipyard lingo for air-conditioning units. Forward of that, a section toward the bow incorporated three bow-thrusters. Four stabilizers, two a side and each within its appropriate *bloc*, were also in place.

Shipyard moves are always scheduled for weekends so as not to discommode the main workforce. Before Friday quitting time, workers cleared the dock floor of all scaffolding and ancillary paraphernalia. Open valves admitted white-frothed river water. After hours of influx, embryonic G32 was quietly afloat.

Then she was winched down the dock, over the step and into position above duplicate keel blocks. Some of them were incredibly elaborate. G32's afterplating rises high above the midship keel level to allow a landing space for the pods. Thus, specific keel structures of gradually increasing height had been fabricated, the aftermost one 46 feet (14 meters) tall. All were topped with U-shaped brackets conforming to the shape of the anticipated stern sections.

In her new position, hawsers locked G32 in place. As the dock drained, she settled down atop her new blocks. Then cherry pickers, utility vehicles, and all the other dry dock impedimenta were lowered back down onto the puddled floor. Forme B would not be inundated again until G32's exit.

Over the months that followed, the hull was shrouded in scaffolding, with welding platforms attached leechlike along her growing flanks. The site was lit inside and out with festoons of shipyard illumination, ropes of high-wattage bulbs burning within white plastic buckets, like a giant's string of Christmas lights. Perpetual welding smoke wreathed the hull, illumined by the flicker of electric arcs. Underfoot was the crunch of red/black rutile, welding's inescapable byproduct. Pedal point for the construction symphony was the clang of a maul deep within the interior and a dissonant fugue of abrasive grinders and screaming cutting wheels. Harbinger of a section move was the warning bell of a gantry moving along its dockside track, unspooling a black rubber umbilical cable as it approached.

Casual shipyard visitors sometimes despaired of seeing G32 grow. On arrival, there she was, the hull they had traveled miles to see, vast, inert, pulsing with light but apparently changeless. Sometimes days passed with no additions and then, unexpectedly, a defining bow or stern section would be gloriously in place. Another puzzle piece had been added and the emergent ship materialized further.

Let us document a sample section installation. Lifts are scheduled only on windless days. Not only is an anemometer vital equipment for the crane operator, but the operations supervisor must remain in touch with the local meteorological office. St.-Nazaire is notorious for violent, unpredictable wind squalls christened *bourrasques* by the locals.

Suspended from the gantry, the lifting cradle—a beam that spreads the load between slings—was positioned over the parked section. Riggers clambered atop it, attached cables to lifting lugs—like steel rabbit ears—and then dismounted. No one ever rides a moving section.

When gantry motors ground into life, the section rose over and then along the hull before stopping above

its appointed destination. It paused while residual swing dissipated and then began its agonizingly slow descent.

Waiting below were ship fitters, including four "pilots," senior men positioned around every side of the landing point. They remained in radio contact with both crane operator and operations supervisor, who stood atop the hull as though on a conductor's podium.

Careful preparations had long been completed around the area of attachment. All bearing points and surfaces had been burnished rust-free. Shipyard lights were deployed atop the area, for daylight would turn to night with the section down. Perhaps the most crucial preparation was placement of guidance yokes, vertical steel posts, fifteen inches (thirty-eight centimeters) high and eight inches (twenty centimeters) square. These uprights were sited around the landing perimeter, first points of sliding contact between descending element and waiting hull. They would lock the section into its precise hovering position, ensuring that its hundreds of tons moved only vertically. Ascertaining the alignment of yokes with descending section was the pilots' responsibility.

Opposite: The overwhelming bulk of Stephen Payne's bridge bloc descends into place. *Above: QM2*'s chic single stack seems light-years removed from original *Mary*'s dignified trio.

High above, gantry controls were operated by digital control. On command, the crane operator punched buttons to produce minuscule electronic pulses, lowering the section almost imperceptibly, fractions of an inch at a time. With the section just above its resting place, binding last-minute adjustments were made with pull jacks, powerful hydraulic jacks that contract rather than expand. Workers operating four pull jacks can align and snug newly joined steel masses together at the last moment. Then welding teams clipped on electrodes, donned masks, and married old and new, bulkhead to deck. Conjoined hull components were doubly welded, inside and out. The formerly independent Lego piece was no longer a solitary honeycomb but an intrinsic component of G32's growing matrix.

In this fashion, the vessel achieved her remarkable height. By mid-March, every bow, stern, and bridge section had been welded in place, save for the final 10-foot (3-meter) topmost funnel courses. That could not be added in Forme B because G32 had risen so high that no clearance remained between crossbeam and superstructure. The funnel-top would be added later.

We should not leave *QM2*'s upper decks without documenting installation of her two gas turbines. The size of a small limousine, each was housed within an acoustically shielded compartment aft of the funnel.

That gas turbine duo atop *QM2* does exactly the same thing as the diesels far below: generates electricity. They burn lighter-weight marine gas oil, a more refined fuel. When *Queen Mary 2* is bunkered, two separate varieties of oil must be pumped aboard.

With no gantry tasks outstanding, G32 could relinquish her place of birth. Two coats of red, anti-foul paint anointed the underwater hull before departure. Masked, goggled, and increasingly spattered, shipyard paint teams deployed on cherry pickers twice sprayed G32's lower plating with a pristine, carmine coat.

The move was scheduled over a March weekend. Rather than mere float-off, this was float-out. Unable to move under her own power, G32 was handled instead by eight tugs. The flotilla assembled offshore before midnight on Thursday, March 20, a nearly windless evening. Forme B had been flooded and G32, a proper ship now, rose again off her blocks. The water continued to flood in and, once interior level matched exterior Loire, Forme B's caisson was shunted aside. Four tugs entered the dock, and made fast fore and aft of their giant charge.

Since generators had been installed on *QM2's* top deck, lights gleamed through every one of the vessel's bridge screen openings, creating the illusion that an operational ship was setting out to sea. Only after the tugs had her firmly in hand were mooring cables slipped. Then, at four o'clock in the morning, G32 was ushered cautiously out into the Loire.

It was a momentous occasion. Despite the hour, Stephen Payne, yard chairman Patrick Boissier, staff from the yard, and inspection teams were on hand. They shared an incredible maritime vision: partially obscured by darkness and only ethereally illuminated, *QM2* was on the move.

Above: Masked workers spray red paint on *Queen Mary 2's* hull, a far cry from the workers who painted the original *Mary* with brushes and buckets. *Opposite: Queen Mary 2,* surrounded by tugboats, casts an eerie glow through the morning fog. *Overleaf:* The morning after her momentous Loire outing, *Queen Mary 2* is again moored at her fitting-out pier. (Photograph by Maurizio Eliseo)

Hull G32

Queen Mary 2 Emerges

Our goal from a marketing point of view is to introduce a whole new generation of travelers to the joys of a transatlantic crossing. You could fly across by air in six hours, but six rewarding days at sea gives you the gracious gift of time—the opportunity to do wonderful things that you never have time for at home.

—Deborah Natansohn, Senior Vice President Marketing & Sales

That brief Loire outing concluded almost immediately with another landfall. Tugs shepherded their charge into Forme C, the yard's largest fitting-out basin. *Queen Mary 2* supplanted G32, her shipyard moniker.

Transfer from Forme B to C permitted a long-anticipated unveiling. For the first time, *Queen Mary 2* could be seen in total from afar, even though still unfinished. Save for an expanse of red underwater hull, the vessel was unpainted, her funnel incomplete, and devoid of lifeboats. It would be late June before the hull's charcoal gray appeared.

Most of the hundreds who came to see her had no idea that vital components were not in place; not one pod was suspended beneath the hull. No Mermaid pods had arrived in St.-Nazaire prior to float-out because of the need to incorporate some late-stage design improvements. Nevertheless, yard officials had implemented the move to Forme C regardless because they had a proverbial ace up their sleeve; Forme C is not merely a basin, it is also a dry dock, although it had not been drained since 1972. Well in advance of float-out, Forme C was drained so that its neglected floor could be strengthened. A new set of keel blocks, tailor-made for Forme C, were set out, placed atop supplementary spreaders that distributed the ship's bulk more evenly.

Then the pods arrived. Each has three elements—propeller, pod, and vertical control element. The combined package weighs 350 tons (317 metric tons), almost the equivalent of a loaded Boeing 747. Consider first the four-bladed, stainless steel props. (All seven *QM2* propellers—four pods and the bow-thruster trio—are made of stainless steel for longer wear.) Their diameter is nearly twenty feet (six meters). Each blade is bolted onto a central boss so that a defective blade can be replaced if necessary.

Since the shaft to which the propeller is attached protrudes from the pods' forward end, *QM2* propellers pull rather than push the vessel, allowing the revolving blades to bite into clean water. For the same reason, the two contrasting sets of pods—the forward fixed pair and the after azimuthing ones, designed to rotate to any direction—are positioned inboard and outboard respectively, preserving the integrity of that clean water flow.

The pod itself is shaped like a miniature submarine or engine nacelle projecting from a blimp. Included

within the vertical control column is a mandatory ladder for inspection purposes, only when in port and not under way. Engineers advise me that maneuvering around a pod's interior requires snakelike agility.

The height of the control columns connecting pod to vessel depends on the location. Those for the fixed pair enter the hull on the underside of Deck A and the height of that deck absorbs the entire column. But the after azimuthing pair requires more substantial anchoring. Since nudging *Queen Mary 2* sideways generates punishing torque, their support columns must project up through Decks A and Deck 1 combined. Acting as *QM2*'s rudder, they are rotated by electric servo-motors through 360 degrees and their turning diameter just clears the central skeg, an exterior keel extension reinforcing the stern's stability.

Late pods notwithstanding, on-board work had to continue; Pam Conover's countdown clock was still ticking relentlessly. The vessel's interiors were merely echoing steel chambers, structurally complete but devoid of decorative cladding. Converting empty shell to finished ship consumed seven months, from May until December 2003, with an August pause as thousands of workers

---

Above: Arriving in Forme C aboard a multi-wheeled transporter, a Mermaid pod is lofted up by crane. *Opposite:* Supported on a stout cradle, a pod is hoisted into place from the dry dock floor. Coordinated inside and out by radioed commands, the propeller and its pod are winched carefully up to position beneath the hull.

departed on their annual vacation. On September 25, nearly four weeks following resumption of work, *Queen Mary 2* departed for builder's sea-trials.

Awaiting *QM2* was a vast accumulation of materiel—scaffolding, ductwork, railings, pipes, decking, and crated glass. Cribs overflowed with ship chandlery—hawsers, chain, lines, paint, shackles—bosun's supplies that bring a ship to life. *Queen Mary 2* was linked to shore by hawsers, gangways, and gargantuan bundles of electric cable and compressed air hose, vital ganglia providing power throughout the vessel.

Every day over the months that followed, nonstop aerial traffic linked ship and shore as well. Four whirly cranes lofted items up from pier-side depot to on-board destinations, their swinging jibs extended to reach the ship while she was further offshore on keel blocks. One early crane task was hoisting aboard final courses for the funnel. They were secured to the truncated funnel stump awaiting them.

That topping-out also included installation of two trumpet-shaped Tyfon whistles, one new, the other on permanent loan from Long Beach's *Queen Mary*. The one originally located in her second funnel had been taken down, crated, and shipped to *Queen Elizabeth 2* for passage from Fort Lauderdale to Southampton and ultimately to St.-Nazaire.

The two whistles are sounded by compressed air on *QM2*, venting a token steam cloud for nostalgic effect. Seven feet (2.13 meters) long and 3 feet (1 + meters) high, each Tyfon weighs a hefty 1400 pounds (633 kilograms). The mechanism's heart is a 22-inch (57-centimeter) diaphragm capable of generating an earth-shattering *basso profundo* blast keyed to low bass A. The *Mary's* and *Elizabeth's* whistles in Southampton and New York were once an evocative, postwar tocsin, and the same majestic reverberations now reecho along both waterfronts.

Moving about *Queen Mary 2* during fitting out demanded stamina and a working knowledge of every

deck's plan. No interior space was easily recognizable, and obstructions, both physical and visual, abounded. Cable and hoses spread like malevolent vines everywhere, crowding staircases with impenetrable tangles that the French call *le jardin des serpents*—the snake garden. Those cable festoons, together with workboxes, paint cans, table saws, pipes, and lumber, ambushed the unwary. Dangling cables and projecting battens underscored the wisdom of ubiquitous signs *Casque Obligatoire*, "Hardhat Necessary".

No elevators functioned, their shafts open, the mechanism of their cars under assault by intent electricians. The only motorized ascent was via industrial lift towers servicing the vessel's starboard flank. Most walked and a constant stream of managers, workers, visitors, and inspection team members plodded up and down staircase towers, improvised hand railings a necessity. Light levels were low, staircases and public rooms alike inadequately illuminated by the familiar giant Christmas tree lights.

There was little finished interior to see, for the vertical grandeur of every double-height space—Grand Lobby, Britannia, Royal Court, Queens Room, Illuminations—was obscured by scaffolding, erected to facilitate finishing work on every ceiling. The promenade desk was a littered, puddled wilderness, the bridge a jumble of cables and gaping consoles. On cold days, chilled zephyrs wafted the length of open-end corridors.

Welcome relief from the huggermugger on board was a restorative tour of finished cabin mockups in a warehouse. Those demonstration cabins are complete save for clients, luggage, and belongings. Everything else is there—beds, mattresses, coverlets, chairs, pillows, curtains, desks, lamps, and a prefabricated bathroom. When the mockups were unveiled, Cunard hotel staff torture-tested everything; no shred of detail or décor escaped their scrutiny. They bounced on beds, worked curtains to distraction, tugged at shower curtains, and wrenched drawers. Mattress and pillow comfort was appraised, closets scrutinized, placement of hooks and shelves debated, and dressing table finish evaluated.

Over summer and early autumn, the on-board chaos relented and recognizable shreds of the ship's interior were gradually revealed. For owners and designers, fitting-out is cumulatively rewarding as long-cherished public room renderings finally emerge to full-blown life. Clean, contoured ceiling appeared atop anonymous gray steel. This was healing and finishing time, the whine of grinding wheel and crackle of arc weld supplanted by the scrape of plasterers' trowels and the slap of paintbrush; mosaic and paneling began covering gloomy steel parameters forever.

Deck surfaces were transformed with bright marble and composition tile, product of dozens of kneeling workmen's patient toil. In the galley, thousands of tiles were laid, separated by stainless steel drainage grids. Only then could ranges, cauldrons, fryers, sinks, dishwashers, mixers, and yards of stainless steel counters be manhandled and plumbed into their assigned positions.

The nature of the on-board work was betrayed by the changing materials spread on the pier, from hardware to house wares: duvets and Frette sheets, Simmons mattresses, boxed chairs, balcony furniture, carpet rolls, bales of curtains and bedspreads, light fixtures, and cartons of towels were hoisted on board.

By fall, interior walls had been sufficiently completed to allow works of art to be mounted. Among the largest was a bas-relief for the Grand Lobby by Scotsman John McKenna. For this, his first shipboard commission, McKenna employed burnished sheet bronze framed with stainless steel. Sited along the wall opposite Grand Lobby's twin panoramic elevators, it is 20 x 23 feet (6 x 7 meters), so large that McKenna relocated to a more capacious Ayrshire studio. He portrays a bow view of *Queen Mary 2*, set against transatlantic sun, clouds, compass rose, and navigational chart. There is also a working clock, incorporated, at the sculptor's recommendation, "within Greenland."

One of McKenna's logistical challenges was transporting the piece to St.-Nazaire. He subdivided it into four component parts, each crated separately for shipping. No such subdivision was necessary for celebrated Dutch artist Barbara Broekman. Her Britannia Restaurant tapestry arrived rolled up, 20 x 30 feet (6 x 9 meters). It depicts a giant Cunarder's bow, neither *Queen Mary 1* nor *2* but an evocative in-between, sailing from New York. Broekman has invigorated her image with an industrial overlay of the 120-year-old Brooklyn

Bridge—"strong, abstract, and very three-dimensional"—conveying precisely the right robust, mechanistic input to buttress her ocean liner vision.

Broekman's design was made into a tapestry at a Polish mill in Posnan on the Gobelin principal. Two teams of four weavers completed the job. The materials employed were wool interwoven with fireproof Trevira, a combination that enriched each color field with a vibrant luster. Broekman's tapestry serves as stunning focal point from both dining room levels, recalling the three photographic tapestries aboard *QE2*. Throughout *QM2*'s life, Broekman's image will serve as backdrop for millions of passenger snapshots. It enriches Britannia Restaurant marvelously, which emerged as one of the vessel's grandest spaces, satisfying every nuance of passenger showmanship. Upper and lower levels are connected by twin, sinuously curving staircases lined with clear glass railings, tailor-made for languid, ceremonial descents.

Four decks higher, the Winter Garden ceiling has been capped with foliated, painted panels executed by London's Ian Cairnie. In preparation for that ceiling canvas, London's Kew Gardens' collection of tropical palms proved an invaluable resource. Banana palm

leaves are Cairnie's main decorative elements; additional fishtail palms and orchids convey the appropriate hot-house ambience.

Another Cairnie *QM2* commission were four pastiches, inspired by seventeenth century Dutch still lives, to enrich the D Staircase, depicting a variety of household silver, china, and linen. Ingeniously, the artist has concealed subtle reproductions of *QM2* logo's within the paintings, engraved on silver or embroidered into linen. What better rainy-day activity for young passengers than to be dispatched on an artistic treasure hunt, searching out the vessel's logo concealed in an otherwise scrupulously re-created Dutch still life?

From still lives to sea lives. Decorating another *QM2* staircase will be thirty canvasses by maritime artist Stephen Card. In fact, though painted on canvas, they are backed with aluminum panels to retain their crispness. Card is a rarity, the world's only maritime painter who also has master's papers; he grew up in Bermuda but now calls Australia home.

Captain Card's work decorates C Staircase all the way from Deck 10 down to Deck 1. Subject matters range from little *Britannia* of 1840 through today's *Queen Mary 2*, embracing intervening *Carpathia*, *Caronia*, *Lusitania*, *Aquitania*, and the three other *Queens*. Passengers descending that main staircase should forsake elevators to savor the impact of that stunning collection.

Opposite: The view aft from the bridge. *Above*: Model-maker Brandwijk lowers the superstructure onto his stunning Commodore Club *QM2* model. A tangle of optic cables fills the interior.

Card is expertly familiar with the structure and history of every vessel he reproduces. Although some ships are seen under way, others are in port, just arrived or about to sail at dusk. The illuminated buildings and the lights of his ships produce a haunting crepuscular vision, perfect décor for *QM2*'s ocean liner ethos.

Yet another and exacting representation of the vessel highlights the Commodore Club: a full hull model of *Queen Mary 2*, the work of Dutch model-maker Henk Brandwijk. Though he normally specializes in reproducing floating originals, *Queen Mary 2* is Brandwijk's first ocean liner commission. The hull is eleven and a half feet (three and a half meters) long, made of oak covered with fiberglass epoxy. Brandwijk fabricates every model element, from lifeboats to railings to deck lights. Windows and portholes are translucent and 2400 fiber-optic cables ensure that they glow, bringing miniature *Queen Mary 2* to glorious, inhabited life.

From wall-mounted works of art to human works of art afoot, another shipboard first: a theatrical company recruited from London's Royal Academy of Dramatic Art. The presence of those young actors offers an opportunity "to see the stars of tomorrow today on *QM2*." Ellis Jones, Executive Director of RADA's New Business Developments, recruited the company; two of his five actors are enjoying their first professional engagement. Also on-board is a graduate with an RADA Diploma in Technical Theatre Arts who serves as combined stage and company manager and also liaises with the cruise staff.

Their maiden production—*Shakespeare's Lovers*—is a compendium of play excerpts interspersed with mono-logues, poems, and madrigals exploring the various aspects of love throughout the Bard's *oeuvre*. Costumes are "simple but effective" and scenery nonexistent; the aim is less spectacle than the spoken word.

Embarkation of this unique acting company is a win/win situation, prize resource for passengers no less than unique employment for talented performers.

Additional works of art afoot bring Royal Court to musical life. Cunard's Director of Entertainment is Englishman Martin Lilly. From his office in Miami, he has signed sufficient singers, dancers, technicians and musi-cians to play within all of *Queen Mary 2*'s entertainment

venues. A nine-piece orchestra tootles in the Royal Court's pit, seven pieces swing-and-sway for Queens Room dancers, a quintet gyrates down in G32, while a jazz trio thumps away in the Commodore Club.

Production shows have been mounted thanks to collaboration between two British firms, Stage Electric and Belinda King Presents. Boasting a prestigious track record, impresario King scoured the world in search of just the right combination of four singers and twelve dancers who make up the Royal Court's company. Just as elements of *Queen Mary 2*'s physical plant were plucked from a global marketplace, so King sought out accomplished Russian ballet dancers as well as knowledgeable Argentinean tangoists.

But however international her search, the Royal Court's theatrical concept is, by intent, purposely homegrown. Adhering firmly to British roots, Cunard's production choices are stamped with a distinctive Mayfairian elegance sea miles removed from cruising's customary norm of Las Vegian glitz.

Finally, works of art at table. *QM2*'s executive chef is a genial Austrian called Karl Winkler, who served in the same capacity aboard *QE2* before assignment to the new flagship. It is an ironic fact of contemporary shipboard's catering life that landlocked Austria produces the majority of today's seagoing chefs. Chef Winkler's menus are enriched by some inspired input from celebrated chef Daniel Boulud. His top-ranked restaurant, Daniel, remains New York gastronomes' favored destination.

Yet another restaurateur, Todd English, has created a restaurant on Deck 8, equivalent venue of original *Queen Mary*'s Veranda Grill. English is a combined chef and entrepreneur, having opened restaurants throughout the United States. His first was Olives, such an enviable 1989 hit that duplicate Olives sprang up

Above: Todd English Grill. *Opposite:* Just aft of the Queens Room is the G32 room, named after *QM2*'s shipyard monicker.

everywhere. Todd's mother was Italian, so his menu preoccupation veers predictably toward the Mediterranean. One hundred and forty-two passengers can be accommodated indoors and—warm-weather bonus—an additional fifty-two can sit out on Deck 8's terrace overlooking the stern, an option more likely to hold sway during *QM2* 's cruising mode.

Sea trials are designed as ultimate tests of every one of the vessel's systems under way. There were two separate trial sessions: a preliminary one in late September called the builder's trials and subsequent owner's trials, which took place in November. That September 25 outing was the first, momentous time that *Queen Mary 2* had ventured out under her own power, departing Forme C solo as a fully functioning vessel. A French master commanded a 400-man shipyard crew. All the vessel's senior officers were aboard in civilian clothes, as were Stephen Payne and both the yard's and Cunard's project managers. Chief Engineer Simon Gillan was particularly thrilled to see the engines that he had coddled for months finally put into full-scale operation.

St.-Nazaire was *en fête*. Crowds thronged the waterfront, hundreds of small craft convoyed the vessel downriver, and five helicopters swarmed overhead and traffic stopped on the suspension bridge as motorists leaned over the railings for a glimpse. As she sounded both Tyfon whistles for the first time, the harbor pilot guided *Queen Mary 2* out the *embouchure de la Loire* where the master set a course southwest toward the Ile de Yeu. *Queen Mary 2* rose easily to the preliminary Biscayan swell, every aspect of her maneuvering behavior absorbed with keenest interest by the Anglo/French teams crowding the bridge.

Over that three-day weekend, forty separate tests were concluded. Anchors were dropped and retrieved, increasing speed was summoned, crash turns were

initiated, full astern essayed, stabilizers initiated then corrected a 9 degree roll and vibration levels were monitored. Although the upper ranges of speed were approached, the dirty hull hampered a true assessment; that would await the owner's November trials. When *Queen Mary 2* returned to St.-Nazaire on Monday morning, Payne was ecstatic. "The first sea trials," he wrote, "were an unqualified success." Successful too for Cunard's public relations department: actual photographs of the ship under way could finally be circulated to the press.

Shipboard's archetypal triad is vessel, crew, and passengers. One pivotal, last-minute embarkation aboard *Queen Mary 2* at St.-Nazaire was 1350 members of her crew. Three hundred and fifty were stewards, the shipboard contingent with whom passengers experience the most telling symbiosis. Although a third had been transferred from *Caronia* and *QE2*, the balance had been recruited anew.

Charged with bringing them up to snuff was Irishman John McGirl. In preparation, three steward recruitment and training centers had been established in Manila, Southampton, and St.-Nazaire. Stewards who had already served aboard Cunarders needed no more than few hours' orientation. But newcomers underwent a rigorous ten-day indoctrination. Neophyte stewards were drilled about menus, and the routine of setting and clearing table, as well as seamless, classic French service.

In early December, incoming crewmembers converged on France, temporarily housed ashore within the myriad holiday camps—untenanted during winter—that dot St.-Nazaire's hinterland. They were not allowed to embark aboard *QM2* until the vessel had been formally handed over from the shipyard's to Cunard's ownership.

Both St.-Nazaire and the shipyard that is its major employer share an understandable pride about the flotillas of glistening new vessels produced at Alstom Chantiers de l'Atlantique. Posters throughout the town proclaim triumphantly: *"St.-Nazaire Construit des Géants"*: St.-Nazaire Builds Giants.

They reflect the combined pride of both corporation and municipality that such an enviable, record-breaking candidate was set sail onto the oceans of the world.

Opposite: The forward stance of *Queen Mary 2* under way is even more impressive than imagined renderings: Stephen Payne's bridge screen is deadly serious. *Above:* Not with her rudder but her two azimuthal Mermaid pods hard over, *Queen Mary 2* executes a sharp turn to port, one of many maneuvers required during sea trials.

Finale & Debut

It was the personal service that made the *Queens* famous, the stewardess, the bedroom steward, the waiter or headwaiter. They were the people that attracted clientele to the Cunard; it wasn't the captain on the bridge, it was the personal service that the passengers used to get.

—Colin Kitching, headwaiter in the original *Mary's* Veranda Grill

Queen Elizabeth 2 and *Queen Mary 2*, Cunard's two consecutive flagships, were scheduled to meet for the first time in New York Harbor on the morning of April 25, 2004, and sail together that evening for Southampton.

Now, after thirty-five years of regular landfalls, *QE2*'s New York calls will be drastically reduced. But during her last transatlantic summer, sad finale was offset by exciting debut as talk of *Queen Mary 2* dominated every conversation. Many of the crew had requested *QM2* transfers, embracing the challenge of the ultimate start-up. Throughout second *Queen Mary*'s galley, for example, *QE2* veterans will abound: 25 percent of the staff had shifted over to *QM2*.

One key player is Cruise Director Ray Rouse. Before showbiz beckoned, he was a London policeman but, in his spare time, a talented amateur dancer. He and his wife Lise were offered professional employment at sea and the post of cruise director followed.

By 2000, Ray had completed seven ship start-ups; then the Beverly Scott Agency telephoned to offer him the *Queen Mary 2* assignment. Rouse is responsible for a cruise staff numbering 15 and in charge of 126 singers, dancers, musicians, and technical personnel.

The vessel's owner's trials took place over a long weekend, November 7 - 11, 2003. With a clean hull and polished propeller blades, *Queen Mary 2*'s official speed was adduced over three consecutive runs with Differential Global Positioning fixes. She averaged 29.62 knots, comfortably exceeding the contractual 29.35. Once, she topped 30.

Back in Forme C, the dock was drained for examination of an errant bow-thruster. Throughout the vessel over those last seven weeks, finishing touches were the order of the day.

Alas, tragedy marred the vessel's final weeks. On Saturday, November 15, a gathering of invited shipyard families assembled for a tour of the vessel. A special gangway rigged to deliver them onto Deck 2 collapsed, causing forty people to fall between the pier and hull. The final toll was appalling: fifteen lives were lost and hospitals within the region were filled with the seriously injured. All of St.-Nazaire, indeed, all of France, was plunged into grief.

Handing a completed vessel over—"delivery" in shipping parlance—remains a brief but significant cer-

emony. On Monday morning, December 22, two maritime/corporate contingents assembled atop the vessel, personnel representing both owner and shipyard.

After some brief preliminary remarks, shipyard chairman Patrick Boissier ordered the French tricolor lowered. Once it was down, Ron Warwick's sole command was "Hoist the red ensign!" The "red duster"—Britain's merchant navy flag—was raised to the mainmast gaff, followed by Cunard's house flag.

That concluded the ceremony, transfer of ownership a *fait accompli*. Eight hundred million dollars worth of ocean liner, a gleaming amalgam of ingenuity, dedication and toil, had been completed and delivered on schedule. Earlier that morning, crewmembers scattered ashore had relinquished temporary French digs to board their new home.

The following day, *QM2* departed. Every pier, mole, and promontory was black with spectators. This was the

Above: Pamela Conover and Commodore Warwick greet Her Majesty, Queen Elizabeth II, as she arrives at the christening. *Opposite:* The Royal Choral Society and the Royal Philharmonic Orchestra perform.

yard finale, as the world's largest passenger vessel departed for her auspicious debut in Southampton. After an "Operation Shakedown and Ship Prep" spell at sea, Captain Warwick turned his vessel's bow north on Christmas morning, bound for the United Kingdom.

Southampton is *Queen Mary 2*'s port of registry and, after her triumphal entry into the port on December 26, she was deluged non-stop with thousands of journalists and travel agents at receptions and overnight excursions.

Climax of that Southampton stay was the christening at 4:00 p.m. January 8, a scrupulously orchestrated occasion months in the planning. Emily Mathieson led the twenty-two strong christening team.

Since England's January weather can be cold and/or wet, a completely outdoor ceremony was out of the question. It had poured rain when first *Queen Mary* had been launched in 1934. So, along an unobstructed, open-air area called the river Test Quay, a completely enclosed auditorium with an ingenious, breakaway wall was erected. Accommodated within would be the launch party, the band of the Royal Marines, the Royal Philharmonic orchestra, the Royal Choral Society, soloists, and seating for 2000 guests.

On her final Southampton entry before the christening, *QM2* remained facing upriver. Once passengers had disembarked, the vessel was inched northward along the Test Quay, bows aligned with the newly-built auditorium.

By my count, *QM2* is the eighteenth ship and sixth passenger vessel Her Majesty has christened over her more than half-century reign. As Princess Elizabeth, Her Royal Highness named Cunarder *Caronia* in 1948. In the mid-fifties, Her Majesty christened *Southern Cross* and the second *Empress of Britain*. In 1967, she named *Queen*

Elizabeth 2, not, as is often thought, after herself but as the second ship named Queen Elizabeth; hence, the vessel's Arabic numeral. Then in 1995, the queen christened Peninsula & Orient's *Oriana*.

The band of the Royal Marines played prior to the ceremony. Then, at 4:05 P.M., the christening party entered: Her Majesty, Prince Philip, Micky Arison, Conover, and newly designated Commodore Ron Warwick. First at the podium was Cunard's President Pamela Conover. She spoke feelingly about her company's pride in the new ship and the signal honor of the royal benison about to be conferred.

Then a four-minute video—*For Queens and Country*—was projected onto twin screens, a splendid recapitulation of the company's recent history. Shown, too, was the Royal Mail's postal banner that would fly from *Queen Mary 2*'s yardarm. As a condition of that privilege, the vessel must embark a token bag of mail for delivery to the United States, perpetuating Samuel Cunard's mandate and entitling the company to use the venerable prefix RMS—Royal Mail Ship—before the vessel's name.

Then, with a stunning coup of theatrical legerdemain, the theater's seaward wall dropped abruptly to reveal the floodlit forepart of *Queen Mary 2*. Pop singer Heather Small serenaded the audience with "Pride" followed by Jim Motherwell, the Queen's personal piper, who played "Amazing Grace" atop the vessel's bow. The hymn was then gloriously reprised by soprano Lesley Garrett.

The Bishop of Winchester, the Right Reverend Michael Scott-Joynt, offered his blessing for the vessel. Within the text of his benediction, he included, *en francais*, a moving acknowledgment of the tragic accident at St.-Nazaire two months earlier.

Finally came the moment for which everyone had been waiting. To the accompaniment of a special Royal Marine fanfare, Commodore Warwick requested Her Majesty's presence at the podium. Then Her Majesty intoned the vessel's proposed name, couched within those time-honored words that have ushered so many immortals into service, "I christen this ship *Queen Mary 2,* and may God bless all who sail in her!" After completing the sentence, she pressed the podium's button. With a crunching pop, three liters of foaming champagne cascaded down *Queen Mary 2*'s bow plating. At the same moment, officer of the watch Tim Armstrong activated a triple, booming salute from the vessel's Tyfon whistles. Before the Queen resumed her seat, the Commodore led three rousing cheers for Her Majesty. *Queen Mary 2,* named by the same sovereign who baptized her predecessor thirty-seven years earlier, had entered formally into service.

January 12, 2004, marked the start of the vessel's maiden voyage to Fort Lauderdale. As they embarked, passengers were greeted by white-gloved stewards and conducted to their cabins. Near sailing time, passengers thronged the vessel's portside railings on both the promenade decks as well as hundreds of balconies, anticipating the moment of departure.

"Queen's weather" held for the departure, cool and dry without the gales predicted by the newspapers. Commodore Warwick, Staff Captain Chris Wells, and the Trinity House pilot Ray Smart were huddled on the port

bridge wing; the red-and-white "H" flag, the pilot's flag, flew from the yardarm. Sheltered from the evening chill by the terminal's doorway, a military band played martial airs. As final cables were slipped and the great black wall of hull glided majestically away from the quay, the strains of "We are Sailing" came plaintively across the water.

The vessel left the pier and, very slowly, proceeded upstream opposite Southampton's Town Quay, surrounded by a flotilla of packed excursion boats, yachts, and small craft. Then QM2 stopped for a final fireworks display, a pyrotechnical salute rocketing up from a barge close by the port side. After the last firework had been fired, Commodore Warwick responded with a booming farewell on his Tyfon whistles to crowds lining the shores of QM2's home port, initiating the maiden voyage to Florida.

There followed a twenty-four-mile, in-harbor passage, Cunard's traditional trail to sea. QM2 passed through Southampton Water and entered the Solent. She passed Cowes to starboard and Portsmouth to port before finally slowing by the Nab Tower.

As the pilot boat cleared away from the hull in a graceful arc for the voyage back up harbor, a flutter of obligatory in-port flags were lowered from high atop QM2. Gathering speed, the liner stood off into the gusty winter night, bearing gently to starboard. Fully victualed and bunkered, RMS *Queen Mary 2* had shrugged off land and returned to her native element, under purposeful way at sea. Micky Arison's vision and Stephen Payne's first line on a piece of drafting paper, initiated five years earlier, had metamorphosed into this incomparably graceful giant breasting Atlantic swells that rolled up-Channel.

Sir Samuel, doubtless absorbing the scene from his celestial vantage point, could not but approve.

Twenty-First Century Cunard Shipboard

Queen Mary 2 Ships that pass in the night are soon forgotten but nights that pass in a ship are remembered forever.

—Anonymous

In 1967, the late Walter Lord, doyen of maritime historians, sailed eastbound as a passenger aboard *Queen Mary*, anxious to witness an event promoted by Cunard as "the last encounter of *Queens* on the Western Ocean."

Mary was already destined for retirement in Long Beach, California, and though *Elizabeth* would soldier on with the *France* for another year, she would also end up stateside, moored in Florida's Port Everglades. Their last joint crossing would bring down the curtain on an unforgettable run, starring two immortals in the most successful transatlantic production ever.

Because of the exigencies of their respective schedules, the *Queens* would meet well after dark. Both masters diverted toward one another, shrinking the sixty-mile gap separating the company's east- and westbound lanes. Walter's notes convey to perfection the mood on board:

"25 September: During the auction pool, word spread that the staff captain had announced that we'd pass the *QE* about 2:15 a.m…Just before 2:00, loudspeaker was announcing that *QE* is 15 miles away…Can see her lights on the horizon…the whole *Mary* is a bedlam…Passengers are pouring out in evening clothes, pajamas, everything…We swarm to the Boat Deck rails, many with cameras… Now the ships are almost abreast…*QE* looks magnificent."

Their bows crossing, the two giants tore past one another, port to port. Both masters sounded their Tyfon whistles simultaneously. Joint salutes racketed across the intervening waves, three blasts overlapping and echoing a fervent response. Passengers along both Boat Deck railings cheered and waved. Hundreds of cameras flashed so that it seemed that the two Clyde-built hulls struck sparks as they raced by. Walter marveled at the brevity of the encounter, as *Queen Elizabeth*, her glittering broadside shrunk into a three-quarters after view and her funnel lights extinguished, vanished into the night as abruptly as she had appeared.

Abruptly, meeting and moment passed, the ultimate "ships that pass in the night." *Queen Mary* and *Queen Elizabeth*, those staunch consorts, would never encounter each other again. For Walter, definitive *Titanic* historian, it had been yet another evocative "night to remember."

Neither captain, the *Mary*'s Treasure Jones nor Geoffrey Marr in command of the *Elizabeth,* could

have guessed that four decades later, another *Mary* and *Elizabeth* would share eastbound passage from New York to Southampton. Rather than farewell, this was joyous transition. *QM2* was assuming the transatlantic mantle relinquished by *QE2*. Henceforth, the second *Mary* would thunder along Cunard's hallowed route while the second *Elizabeth* would revert to cruising out of Southampton. This *Mary* and *Elizabeth* would re-meet time and again, either in Southampton, the Mediterranean, the Caribbean or, each December, in mid-Atlantic, out of sight but reassuringly on station.

How long will *Queen Elizabeth 2* remain in service? No one knows. But presumably, her world cruises may one day be co-opted by Panamax' *Queen Victoria*. Stephen Payne assures us that *Queen Mary 2* will be with us until the mid-twenty-first century. Moreover, this giant new flagship can call at 95 percent of the ports used by her predecessor.

This chapter's "history" must be predicted rather than recorded. Obviously, she will show Cunard's flag proudly throughout the world. During her maiden Caribbean foray in early 2004, she sails to Rio de Janeiro—just as *Aquitania* had in 1938—offering four giddy days of carnival. En route she crosses the equator, rewarding her passengers with an historic first: King

Above: The scene on *Queen Mary 2*'s bridge at the start of passage to Southampton. *Opposite:* Lying peacefully in late afternoon sun, *QM2*'s charcoal gray hull glows with the setting sun.

Neptune—cruise director Ray Rouse complete with trident and cotton wool beard—inducted nervous, newcomer "pollywogs" hilariously into his domain.

I can envision *Queen Mary 2* during summertime Mediterranean jaunts, berthed beneath Gibraltar's looming Rock or tied up alongside at Mussolini's mid-thirties Neapolitan terminal. In Venice, her record-breaking bulk will help fill the *Statzioni Maritima,* permitting her passengers an incomparable Venetian idyll. In the Caribbean, I picture her anchored out off St. Thomas, tendering passengers ashore or moored alongside at Barbados beneath subtropical skies but cool withal. In high summer, *QM2* will trace Norway's rugged coastline, rejoicing in unreal midnight sunlight and turning about the North Cape's forbidding eminence.

One unforgettable long voyage could surpass Rio's southernmost latitude of the inaugural season. Ron Warwick's great regret is that, throughout his long seagoing career, he never sailed around the Horn. Given the inability of post-Panamax *Queen Mary 2* to transit the canal, it is not inconceivable that one day both vessel and her master might undertake that historic passage together. Not only a memorable voyage, it would also permit an encounter between the two *Queen Mary*s in Long Beach; there could follow a triumphant Pacific tour, encompassing California, Hawaii, and all those exotic Far Eastern ports of call.

But unquestionably, the most endearing vision is *Queen Mary 2* in mid-Atlantic, basking in that exhilaratingly detached limbo between continents, bound on a crossing that will end either with majestic progression up the North River to Manhattan or wending her way past Cowes inbound to Southampton and home. For it is out there, in Cunard country, that the vessel delivers her most rewarding promise. Rather than moored alongside some tempting littoral, the great liner is where she belongs, under way.

How will her human cargo behave throughout their crossing? They will do, on the one hand, exactly what their forebears did aboard nineteenth- and twentieth-

century Cunarders. On the other, they will enjoy richer and more varied sea days, exploring and expropriating the delights of what Deborah Natansohn has described so cogently as their "feature-rich" vessel.

Share a bird's-eye view. At break of day, along serried balcony rows, white-robed passenger couples survey the sea, restorative coffee to hand. Along both sides of Deck 7, early-morning walkers tramp their appointed circuits. Those laps complete, they and treadmill addicts from the gym join fellow passengers in the morning brightness of Britannia Restaurant, where the slanting sun strikes prismatic sparks from crystal glasses. Up in the King's Court, other early-bird passengers congregate, drawn by that irresistible sensory amalgam of coffee, bacon, and fresh bread. Up behind the bridge, master, staff captain, chief engineer, and hotel manager gather for a Captain's meeting to discuss the day's events.

Once crewmen have hosed down the teak, deck stewards organize daytime chair ranks. Since the weather is sunny but bracing, ready to hand are stacks of Cunard's double-weight, blue-red steamer rugs, perfect for shrouding outdoor readers and dreamers against that glaring, mid-ocean chill.

Forward on Deck 3, ConneXions is astir as avid e-mailers scroll through overnight arrivals, while others take chairs to learn some French or, kindness

Opposite: With tables set, the Britannia Restaurant awaits its first guests. (© Michel Verdure) *Above:* The Holyrood Suite is the middle of the three duplex apartments on Decks 9 and 10 in the stern. (© Michel Verdure)

of an obliging Oxford don, the glories of Gothic architecture. Junior passengers corralled aft on Deck 6 are distracted with scissors, paste, and Crayola but soon clamor for the morning's scavenger hunt to begin.

Mid-morning in the Winter Garden, passersby sip bouillon and ponder the daily quiz. Up one deck forward, the librarian helps a passenger track down an elusive biography, careful not to disturb postcard writers with bowed heads scribbling their quota. Five decks down in the casino, a solitary but determined matutinal gambler engages a promising slot.

On Deck 1, there is other play within the hushed purlieus of Kensington as bridge devotees absorb a lecture before being dealt the first of many hands of duplicate. Inveterate shoppers stroll throughout Deck 3's inviting shops; one tries on a Chanel jacket, another evaluates canisters of Harrods tea, a third samples yet again a bewitching perfume, and a couple lingers wistfully over a seductive bauble in the jewelry display case.

Lunch beckons, and friends with a birthday in mind quaff a preliminary glass in the Veuve-Clicquot Champagne Bar; they have already booked a Todd English table for full-blown celebration that evening. The Canyon Ranch SpaClub almost empties out as the midday meal approaches, save for a residue of sybarites who prolong their soporific soak in the pool.

There is a brisk preprandial cocktail trade up in the Commodore Club, every window table full as passengers enjoy the hypnotic spectacle of *Queen Mary*'s white prow forging effortlessly ahead. Atop the vessel, newly risen teenagers crowd the Boardwalk Café in quest of a pizza or hamburger breakfast. The retractable glass roof just forward is sealed against ocean winds, and, throughout the day, pool waters are roiled by swimmers and their ship's motion alike.

As the sun reaches its zenith, chatter in every dining room is momentarily quelled as Captain Warwick broadcasts noontime details of the vessel's position and performance. Somewhere on board, the winner of the announced mileage pool cannot suppress a cry of delight.

During the afternoon, the pace slows perceptibly. Though siesta's siren song lures the susceptible to cabin or sheltered deck chair, dogged work continues in the gym. A feature film is scheduled in Illuminations while more erudite fare emanates from adjacent ConneXions. Tea awaits in the Winter Garden, and Queens Grill habitués, rug-bundled and cherishing tea tray in lap, gather peacefully on their stern aerie above the wake.

At sunset, it is time to dress. First sitting passengers in evening finery cross paths with second sitting shipmates relinquishing pool and deck chair. Deck 3's bars are awash with mid-ocean's well-dressed clientele. Some anticipate dinner with a pint in the Golden Lion, others with one of the Chart Room's icy martinis, yet others a flute of Veuve-Clicquot to wash down some Beluga. Down the Grand Lobby's staircase crescent, the casino is open for full-scale gaming. Black-tied dealers await a flood of evening punters, and the roulette wheel's hypnotic rotation begins.

But before submitting to that endlessly captivating risk indulgence, every soul on board is preoccupied with the approaching dinner hour. All restaurant stewards are assembled in evening rig. In King's Court, wall panels and lights have been deployed into evening mode, transforming lido into bistro quartet. A sous-chef and his ingredients are ready in the Chef's Galley, where thirty-five chairs await lucky passengers for a soon-to-be-consumed cookery demonstration. On Deck 3, Britannia's tailcoated *maitre d'hotel* welcomes diners into his white-gloved domain. In the Queens Grill, his equivalent, resplendent Robert Cheadle, conducts his passengers to their chairs.

Forward in the Royal Court, dancers already made up for *Zing Went the Strings* check their costume changes, musicians tune up in the pit, and technicians preset that evening's light plot. The Illuminations projectionist has rewound every reel of his matinee screening and the planetarium dome has been lowered into place for a celestial display. In the Queen's Room, RADA's repertory company is poised for the first of two performances of a Stoppard one-act. In the interim, music prevails as the band plays for couples flocking onto the dance floor.

Throughout those evenings, familiar transatlantic magic prevails. Passengers stroll languidly from one great public room to the next, encountering old friends and making new ones, chatting and laughing, rejoicing in that special contentment engendered by civilized shipboard. Here is indeed a veritable *tableau*

vivant, simulacrum of those virtual reality renderings imagined by company planners long before the vessel's keel was laid.

Some shipmates will stay up long after the shows are over, either as part of the boisterous crowd surrounding the casino's crap table or gathered for a nightcap in the G32 discotheque. A couple or two will reenter from the promenade deck, hair windblown and the man's dinner jacket protecting his companion's bare shoulders. Theirs has been an excursion in quest of a moon or at least a rail-side vigil, watching the white/black waves surge past, turmoil revealed by the illuminated spill from a thousand portholes. "Beyond the green baize door" down in crew country, newly off-duty crewmen and -women throng the Pig & Whistle for a relaxing pint and a gossip.

All will end their evenings with a cabin retreat, where curtains are drawn, lamps aglow and covers turned down. Once in bed, there can be no better day's finale than a glance at tomorrow's program, a televised movie or a bit of a chapter before complete, Morphean surrender.

Her passengers asleep or at play, *Queen Mary 2* perseveres across a gusty Atlantic, remorseless and impervious

to regret. Vigilant officers on the bridge or manning the engine control room monitor the liner's progress and systems, legatees of Sir Samuel's mid-nineteenth century exemplars, guardians of a million passenger dreams.

Coincidentally, millions figure at both beginnings and ends of venerable Cunarders. One proud statistic promulgated when first *Queen Mary* was under construction cited the ten million rivets stitching her hull plates together. And conversely, when *Aquitania* was withdrawn in 1950, it was reckoned just as proudly that, over thirty-six years of service, "Old Reliable" had steamed three million nautical miles.

Millions of rivets, millions of miles—perfect maritime bookends and testament to the inherent strength and longevity of Cunard tonnage. Though Stephen Payne assures that no rivets adorn *Queen Mary 2*'s all-welded hull, the cumulative mileage achieved by this latest flagship over her forty-year life span will easily exceed *Aquitania*'s figurative odometer.

How better to conclude, for this French-built vessel, than with a neat Gallic epigraph. Parisians appraising a newcomer's quality will murmur approvingly "*Bon chic, bon genre*," (good style, good breeding), dual attributes suggesting elegant turnout no less than flawless character.

The same seems gloriously apropos for *Queen Mary 2* —the *bon chic* of her profile and stunning interiors no less than the *bon genre* reliability of her sturdy, seagoing genes. *Bon chic, bon genre*: That gleaming patina atop reassuring steel characterizes to perfection this grandest ocean liner of all time.

Above: It is such a pleasure to read Cunard's port of registry; rather than a flag of convenience, a flag of tradition. *Overleaf:* Robert Lloyd's specially commissioned portrait of *Queen Mary 2* shows her in company with three immortal predecessors, *Elizabeth* on the left, *QE2* and the first *Mary* on the right.

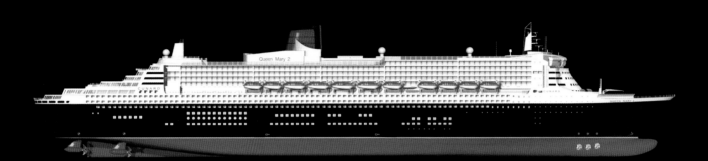

About the QM2:

Length: 1132 feet

Beam: 135 feet

Beam at Bridge Wings: 164 feet

Draft: 32.8 feet

Height (Keel to Funnel): 236.2 feet

Gross Registered Tonnage: Approximately 150,000 tons

Passengers: 2620 double occupancy

Crew: 1254

Top Speed: Approximately 30 knots (34.5 mph)

Power: 157,000 horsepower

Environmentally friendly, gas turbine/diesel electric plant

Propulsion: Four pods of 21.5 MW each: 2 fixed and 2 azimuthing

Strength: Extra thick steel hull for strength and stability for Atlantic trade

Stabilizers: Two sets

Cost: 780 million dollars

Some comparisons:

QM2 is five times longer than Cunard's first ship, *Britannia* (230 ft.)

QM2 is more than twice as long as the Washington Monument is tall (550 ft.)

QM2 is 147 feet longer than the Eiffel Tower is tall (984 ft.)

QM2 is more than 3.5 times as long as Westminster Tower (Big Ben) is high (310 ft.)

QM2 is only 117 feet shorter than the Empire State Building is tall (1248 ft.)

QM2 is more than three times as long as St. Paul's Cathedral is tall (366 ft.)

QM2 is as long as 36 double-decker London buses (31.5 ft. each)

QM2's whistles will be audible for ten miles.

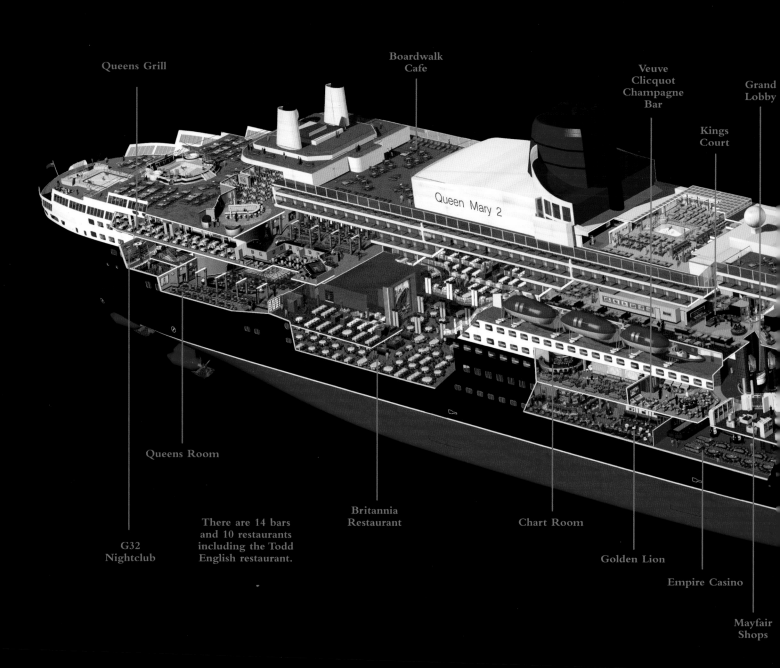

Queens Grill

Boardwalk Cafe

Veuve Clicquot Champagne Bar

Grand Lobby

Kings Court

Queen Mary 2

Queens Room

G32 Nightclub

There are 14 bars and 10 restaurants including the Todd English restaurant.

Britannia Restaurant

Chart Room

Golden Lion

Empire Casino

Mayfair Shops

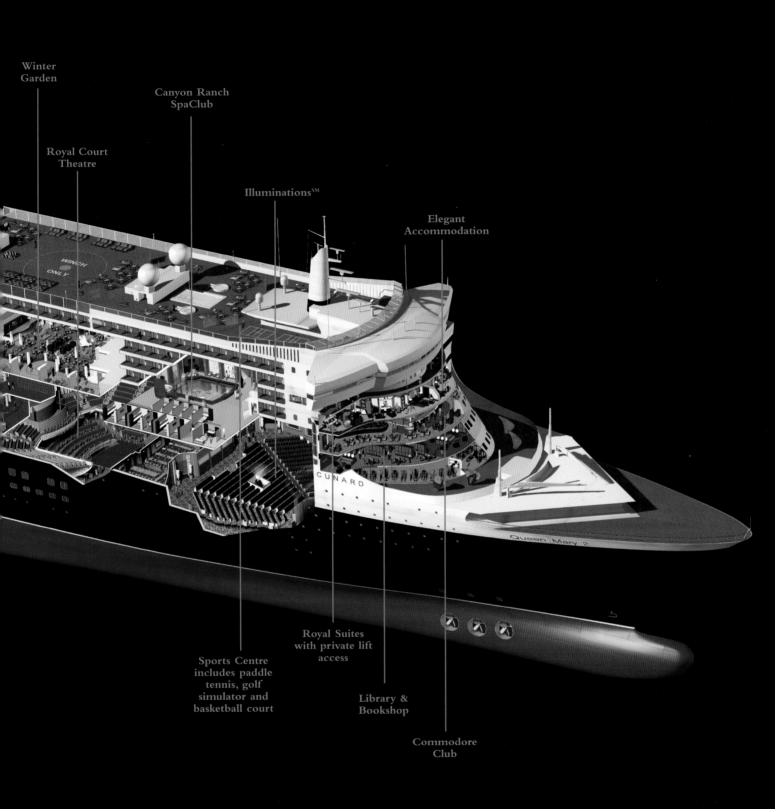

Winter
Garden

Canyon Ranch
SpaClub

Royal Court
Theatre

Illuminations℠

Elegant
Accommodation

WINCH
ONLY

CUNARD

Queen Mary 2

Sports Centre
includes paddle
tennis, golf
simulator and
basketball court

Royal Suites
with private lift
access

Library &
Bookshop

Commodore
Club

Q1	Grand Duplex
Q2	Duplex Apartments
	Queen Mary & Elizabeth Suites
Q3	Royal Suites
Q4	Penthouse
Q5	Suites
Q6	Suites
P1	Junior Suites
P2	Junior Suites
B1	Deluxe Balcony
B2	Deluxe Balcony
B3	Deluxe Balcony*
B4	Premium Balcony
B5	Premium Balcony
B6	Premium Balcony
B7	Premium Balcony
C1	Standard Oceanview
C2	Standard Oceanview
C3	Standard Oceanview
C4	Standard Oceanview
D1	Atrium
D2	Standard Inside
D3	Standard Inside
D4	Standard Inside
D5	Standard Inside
D6	Standard Inside
■	Wheelchair accessible
+	3rd berth is a single sofabed
●	3rd & 4th berth is a double sofabed
✳	3rd & 4th berth are two upper beds

Country of Registry: Great Britain
Gross Tonnage: 150,000 GRT
Length: 1,132 feet
Width: 135 feet
Draft: 32.8 feet

The following decks are not shown:
Deck 1   Includes Medical Center &
          Tender Embarkation Lounges
Deck 3L Includes lower-level G32,
          Art Gallery, Photo Gallery,
          Indoor Promenade & access
          to Queens Room
Deck 13 Includes the Sun Deck, Splash
          Pool & Sports Center

★ Partially obstructed views

Ship deck plans are for illustration purposes only.
Actual cabins may vary, decks are not to scale.

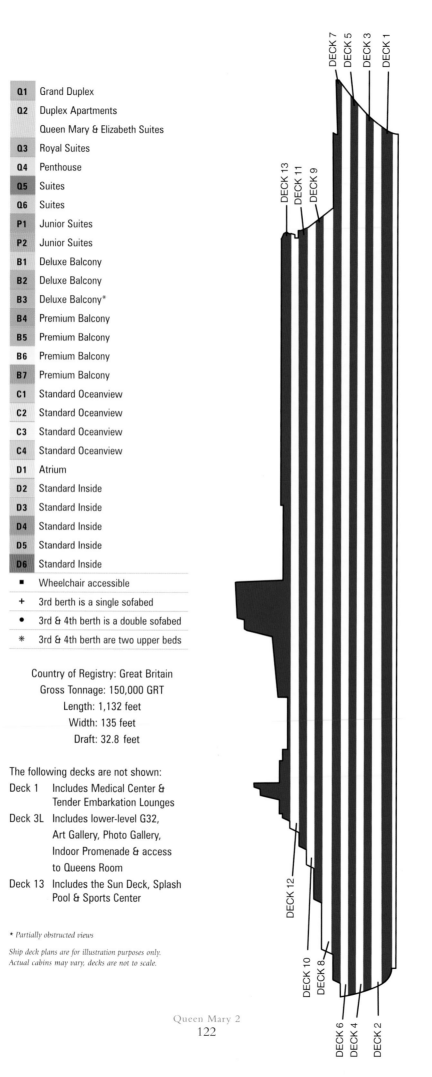

Deck 13 Deck 12 Deck 11 Deck 10

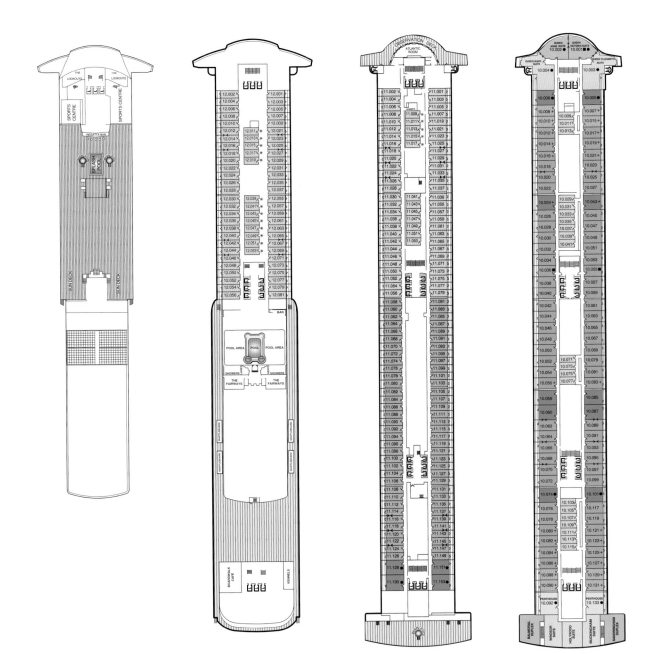

Deck 9

Deck 8

Deck 7

Deck 6

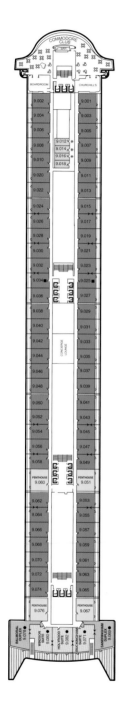
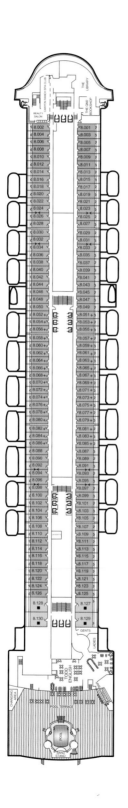
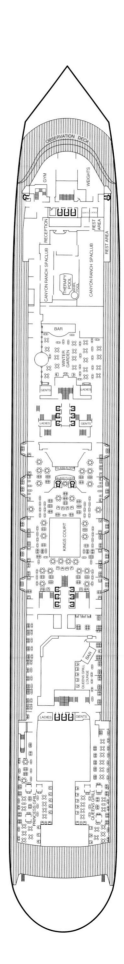

Deck 5

Deck 4

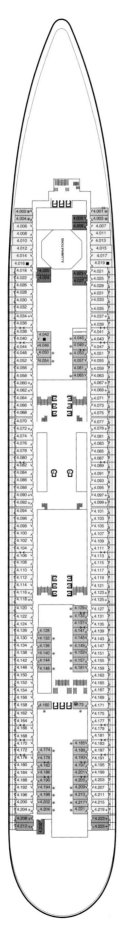

Deck 3

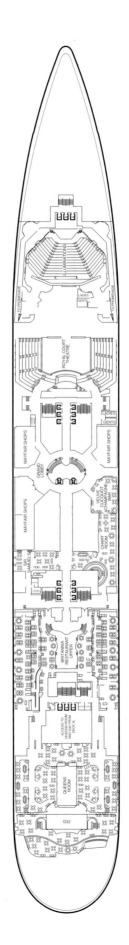

Deck 2

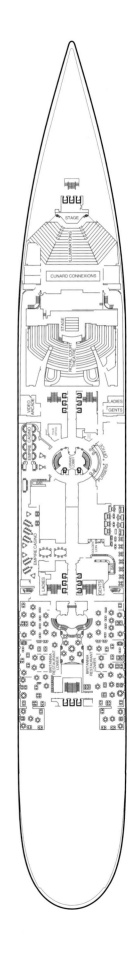

Bibliography

Archer, W. J. *Cruising in the Mediterranean*. London: Jarrolds Limited. 1935

Bailey, Chris Howard. *Down the Burma Road*. Southampton: Oral History Team Southampton Local Studies Section. n.d.

Blake, George. *Queen Mary: A Record in Pictures—1930-1936*. London: B. T. Batsford Ltd. n.d.

Brinnin, John Malcolm and Kenneth Gaulin. *Transatlantiques*. Paris: Editions Robert Laffont. 1989

Brooks, Clive. *Atlantic Queens*. Sparkford: Haynes Publishing Group. 1989

Dodman, Frank. *Ships of the Cunard Line*. London: Adlard Coles Ltd. 1955

De Kerbrech, Richard P. and David Williams. *Cunard White Star Liners of the 1930's*. London: Conway Maritime Press. 1988

Diggle, Captain E. G. *The Romance of a Modern Liner*. London: Sampson Low, Marston & Co., Ltd. 1930

Ellery, David. *RMS Queen Mary*. Dorset: Waterfront Publications. 1994

Hughes, Tom. *The Blue Riband of the Atlantic*. New York: Charles Scribner's Sons. 1973

Hutchings, David F. *Caronia: Legacy of A Pretty Sister*. Market Drayton: Shipping Books Press. 2000

Kaasmann, Herb. *Oregon: Greyhound of the Atlantic*. Clark: Commercial Graphics, Inc. 1993

Lacey, Robert. *The Queens of the North Atlantic*. New York: Stein and Day. 1976

Maxtone-Graham John. *Crossing & Cruising*. New York: Charles Scribner's Sons. 1992

—*Cunard, 150 Glorious Years*. London: David & Charles. 1989

—*The Only Way to Cross*. New York: Macmillan. 1972

—*Tribute to a Queen*. Lausanne: Berlitz Publications. 1987

McCutcheon, Janette. *RMS Queen Elizabeth*. Stroud: Tempus Publishing Limited. 2001

Miller, William H. *Famous Ocean Liners*. Wellingborough: Patrick Stephens. 1987

—and Luis Miguel Correia. *RMS Queen Elizabeth 2 of 1969*. Lisbon: Liner Books. 1999

Potter, Neil and Jack Frost. *The Mary*. London: George G. Harrrap & Co Ltd. 1969

—*The Elizabeth*. London: George G. Harrap & Co. Ltd. 1965

—*Queen Elizabeth 2*. London: George G. Harrap & Co. Ltd. 1969

Prior, Rupert. *Ocean Liners*. London: Tiger Books International. 1993

Smith, Ken. *Mauretania: Pride of the Tyne*. Newcastle: Swan Hunter (Tyneside) Ltd. 1997

Spratt, H. Philip. *Transatlantic Paddle Steamers*. Glasgow: Brown, Son & Ferguson, Limited. 1951

Stevens, Leonard A. *The Elizabeth: Passage of a Queen*. New York: Alfred A. Knopf. 1968

Steel, James. *Queen Mary*. London: Phaidon. 1995

Tyler, David Budlong. *Steam Conquers the Atlantic*. New York: D. Appleton-Century Company. 1939

Warwick, Captain Ronald W. *QE2*. New York: W. W. Norton. 1993

Watt, D.S. and Raymond Birt. *The Queen Elizabeth*. London: Winchester Publications. 1947

Williams, David L. *Glory Days: Cunard*. Hersham: Ian Allan Publishing. 1998

—*Southampton*. Runnymede. Ian Allan Ltd. 1984

Winter, C. R. *The Queen Mary*. New York: W. W. Norton. 1996

Photographing an Icon

I walk the half finished Colossus, hear the crash, whang and clang of raw steel hammered, jammed and wrenched into the hull, the hiss and fiery crackle of hundreds of welders. Deck atop deck, every red or grey steel wall bears chalk scribbles, hieroglyphs for the thousands of hard-hatted workmen to read and interpret. Rough steel staircases march on an on into the sky. Vast enclosed spaces bear a chaos of tubes, wires, pipes, and silver-colored boxes strewn about in seemingly random fashion.

Dusk: I stand on a stone ledge. Below me, a shining bulbous bow large enough to house an aquarium squats attached beneath the unfinished prow. It seems an eye beneath the waves, a blunt tool to cut the wake of white waters and smooth QM2's passage. A grey and infinite illusion, the vast steel hull and superstructure stretch endlessly towards a bleak white sun. Beyond, twin pyramids of a slender high bridge gleam through a pale curtain of early morning mist.

That was the beginning. The bow designed to smooth her passage will vanish beneath the sea, to reappear like a dolphin now and then as *QM2* plows the waves. After twenty years of photographing ocean liners and cruise ships around the world, I feel as one who has caught the golden ring. Could I have been at the birth of the Great Pyramid at Giza or watched the Empire State Building rise, I would have felt the same tingling exuberance. In making this book, I have been privileged to watch and photograph the implementation and construction of a modern marvel.

QM2 is unrivalled in size, cost and luxury. What seduces me are her graceful lines, for a ship is a woman and you must fall in love with her to capture her beauty. Like ballet dancer Suzanne Farrell on point making lovely arabesques in the air, *QM2* will shed her grace on the seven seas. In Shakespeare's words from *Cleopatra*, "She makes hungry where most she satisfies." A great ocean liner becomes a legend in her time. *QM2*, I wish you fair winds on the sea roads of history.

Technical Information: My photographs were made with Canon EOS1n film cameras, and EOS1D and EOS1Ds digital cameras.

Harvey Lloyd
www.harveylloyd.com

Acknowledgments

I am indebted to a host of people, foremost among them my publisher Ross Eberman, whose patience, determination, and ingenuity inspire profound gratitude. I must also thank Harvey Lloyd for his extraordinary photographs, and my dear wife Mary for both her wisdom and support.

Other names follow, listed alphabetically and, I trust, completely: Micky Arison, Patrick Boissier, Edie Bornstein, Daniel Boulud, Barbara Broekman, Louis-Philippe Capelle, Stephen Card, Jill Cohen, Andy Collier, Pamela Conover, Julie Davis, Gerry Ellis, Todd English, Joe Farcus, Eric Flounders, Tim Frew, Jeff Frier, Michael Gallagher, Tim Gallagher, Jean-Jacques Gatepaille, David Gevanthor, Joanna Goebel, Milton Gonzalez, John Grace, Yves Guillotin, Rob Hall, Bill Havens, Martin Hegarty, Erik Hermida, Jacqui Hodgson, Kathy Howard, Isabelle Huyghe, Brenton Jenkins, Fredrik Johansson, Ellis Jones, Philippe Kasse, Bård Kolltveit, Soren Krogsgaard, Kirsten Leonard, Eric Lewis, Martin Lilly, Richard Lloyd, Robert Lloyd, Emily Mathieson, John McGirl, Chantal Mooiman, Karl Muhlberger, Sture Myrmell, Deborah Natansohn, Dick Owsiany, Stephen Payne, James Rae, Captain William Range, Larry Rapp, Robert Reynolds, Ray Rouse, Michael Sand, Linda Schultes, Captain Raymond Smart, Martin Stenzel, Frank Symeou, Mary Thomas, Robert & Tomas Tillberg, Jean Vance-Andrews, Jean-Remy Villageois, Commodore Ron Warwick, Maureen Watry, Rosemary Watt, Brian Wattling, Chris Wells, Barry Winiker, Karl Winkler, Captain Paul Wright, and Letha Wulf.

If any have been inadvertently omitted, my deepest apologies.

John Maxtone-Graham

Editors: Kirsten Leonard, Tim Frew,
  Jean Andrews
Production Coordinator: Joanna Goebel
Production Manager: Richard L. Owsiany
Carpe Diem Books: Ross Eberman, President
  www.carpediembooks.com

Photo Credits

The publisher extends its appreciation to photographer Harvey Lloyd and to everyone else who helped to make this book possible, in particular to Michel Verdure and Yves Guillotin / Chantiers de l'Atlantique. Special thanks also to John Maxtone-Graham and Maureen Watry / The University of Liverpool for the historical images; and to Rob Hall & The Open Agency, Three Blind Mice, and Cunard Line. Several others provided remarkable images, and all contributors are listed below.

© Harvey Lloyd
Pages 15, 17 (right), 18 (left), 19, 20, 24–25, 27, 28, 39, 73, 90, 92–93, 96, 99, 100, 110, 114, 115, and front cover.

© Michael Verdure
Pages 10, 31, 35, 36, 40, 41, 42, 43, 102, 103, 111, 112, and 113.

Courtesy of Chantiers de l'Atlantique
Pages 4–5, 7, 8–9, 16, 18 (right) 23, 26, 29, 44, 81, 82, 84–85, 86, 88, 95, 104, and 105.

Courtesy of Author's Collection
Pages 13, 21, 46, 48, 51, 52, 56 (left), 59, 60–61, 62, 66, 68–69, 70 (top left and right and bottom), 71, 72, 75, 76 (right) 79, 83 (left and right), and 116–117 (painting by Robert Lloyd, by permission of John Maxtone-Graham).

Courtesy of Cunard Line
Pages 32, 38, 47, 77, 118–125; page 45 (photo by Doug Castenado); pages 106, 107, 108, and 109 (photos by Simon Wright).

Courtesy of the University of Liverpool Library
Pages 33, 53, 55, 57, 64, and 65.

© Louis-Philippe Capelle
Pages 94 and 98.

© John Grace
Page 22 and 89.

Courtesy of William Archibald
Page 78.

Courtesy of Henk Brandwijk
Page 101.

Courtesy of Carnival Corporation
Page 17 (left).

Courtesy of Maurizio Eliseo
Page 91.

Courtesy of English Heritage NMR
Page 63.

Courtesy of Mary Evans Picture Library
Page 56 (right).

Courtesy of MARIN
Page 21.

Courtesy of the Queen Elizabeth/ Seawise University Historical Collection
Page 67.

Courtesy of R.M.S. Queen Mary Foundation
Pages 76 (left) and 97.

Courtesy of Tillberg Design
Page 34.

Courtesy of TWBA/Chiat Day
Page 33 (photo by Larry Fink)